The Road To The Great Cosmic Mother

Other Divine Creations by Avivah V.E. Moreland El

Divine Visions Journal—The Journal for Divine Visioneers with eyes to see the unseen.
How Great Thou Art—An art instruction book for children of all ages
The New Ancient Goddess—A Photo Album of the Goddesses
Hand Sculptured Art Greeting Cards of Goddesses
All work copyright 2007 Avivah V.E. Moreland El

The Road To The Great Cosmic Mother

◆

The Soulful Stories and Memoirs of a Goddess

Avivah V. E. Moreland El

iUniverse, Inc.
New York Lincoln Shanghai

The Road To The Great Cosmic Mother
The Soulful Stories and Memoirs of a Goddess

iUniverse books may be ordered through booksellers or by contacting:

iUniverse
2021 Pine Lake Road, Suite 100
Lincoln, NE 68512
www.iuniverse.com
1-800-Authors (1-800-288-4677)

Because of the dynamic nature of the Internet, any Web addresses or links contained in this book may have changed since publication and may no longer be valid.

The views expressed in this work are solely those of the author and do not necessarily reflect the views of the publisher, and the publisher hereby disclaims any responsibility for them.

ISBN: 978-0-595-46071-7 (pbk)
ISBN: 978-0-595-90369-6 (ebk)

Printed in the United States of America

Contents

Gratitude and Acknowledgements

Giving honor and gratitude to:

The Great Cosmic Mother, for the fortitude to keep walking, talking and writing to share truth with others.

My immediate powerful family of women who all willingly and lovingly inspire me moment by moment:

My Great-Great Grandmother Louisa, Great-Grandmother Fannie, Grandmother Fannie Louise and Mother Fannie Andrew Fuller-Moreland are the great lineage who made me.

With my wonderful sisters, Jacqueline and Linda, and brilliant children, Christopher and Monique empower me to be a great role model.

My Granddaughters Kerrington and Tierra are my Young Goddesses that keep me pressing on.

I acknowledge and celebrate "Thanksgiving" and "Valiant Times Day" everyday, for a brave and resilient people that have helped to bring me through and keep pushing me on, from the first ancestor to the present ones and those mentioned above and my childhood playmate and friend Gill McBride, for her being with me since we were three. Jennie Trotter, Founder of the Wholistic Stress Institute of Atlanta for her generous support, my sister friends, Mrs. Maryah Nimetullah for her personal assistance and Arnita Taylor for her technical support on this submission, Melva Pugh for organizing my book review party, my Yogi Brother, Naturopathic healer, and CSA Minister, Samuel Sasu, of Ghana, West Africa who has shown me my true love for natural healing.

Thanks to Rev. Dr. Barbara King, for awakening my Christ consciousness in Metaphysics and knowing The Power Within.

Honor to Paramahansa Yogananda and the Guru line, Reverend Roy Eugene Davis, direct Disciple of Paramahansa Yogananda, and Founder for Center for Spiritual Awareness in Lakemont, Georgia, who initiated me into Kriya Yoga and guiding my actions to be God focused. Thank you Sai Baba for your Pure Love.

I acknowledge Baba Medahochi for revealing the presence of The Great Matriarchal force around me, in me, as me. May his Shamanic work forever dwell in our hearts. To the council of the private Universal Cosmic Motherhood Association (UCMA)

I graciously acknowledge also my top great artists and favorite healers: Maya Angelou for her tone with her spoken words, Oprah for her momentum presence, Toni Morrison and Alice Walker for their gift of writing in color, Jessie Norman and Gil Scott for their gift of conveying music with words, Frankie Beverly for music in great celebration, Tyler Perry for seeing straight into his Great Self, Denzel for adding debonair to the dance of life and who gives me the greatest internal healing massage from ecstatic laughter, Martin Lawrence.

Impressions of the Author

In these pages are the sacred writings, stories and the Soulful Memoirs of a beautiful Goddess's journey in search of absolute peace, perfect love and power, external to herself. The memoirs of The Garden of Eve, The Aura of Love, and the memoir of a Kemetian Initiation describe some of her glimpses of awakening. During her walk, she encountered the path of a traditional, ancient "way" that invokes the Divine Spiritual nature of the cosmos through the assembly of her ancestral line. A gateway to the Supreme state of consciousness resides there in the ultimate of wholeness, the undivided male and female equilibrium.

There is now, upon the earth, an ancient spirit with the appearance of male energy dominance. Today's religion has erroneously and purposely portrayed The Supreme Being as Father, implying a masculine form, "Man" and an invisible spirit, a holy ghost, with an imbalanced flow of energy moving in the earth. To refer to the Supreme as man, creates a cloud for the discerning mind, of an important factor being left out of the whole equation and that is the "Woman". There is in fact mentioned in one of the "Holy" books, The Holy Bible, in the first chapter of Genesis, that Adam named his wife Eve, "The Mother of all living." The femininity of energy is commonly known as the ruling energy in that creation comes out of it and the opposite attention is upon a spiritual force called God. I prefer to reference God as Goddess, since there seems to be an importance with the patriarchal. It has been almost impossible to conceptualize the vastness of this Creative Intelligence. But what has occurred over time is simply the knowledge that there is an entity that is determined to deny, devein and destroy the Truth. In the physical form, there is a way to relate in an all inclusive manner towards one another. I say we *are* Spirit Beings having physical experiences through these embodiments simply because nobody can see just "what makes us tick". Jokingly, we all could see "Casper, the friendly Ghost".

The equal balance of masculine and feminine energy that brings balance and harmony to life is what we all are in such deep desire for in our personal lives and for the planet we live on. I say, only the Great Cosmic Mother can bring that back to Life, when it is allowed. Remembering there is power in what we say, think and do, I say, only The Woman who knows she is the Great Cosmic

Mother will be who straightens this earth out as the World President if there has to be one. Her office is already oval. She won't need defense or homeland security, for there is nothing to fear and plenty to share. Could it be "man's" greatest fear that he won't have anything to be Controler of and Chief of. Many religions of the patriarchal society have silenced the feminine energy even though it is through her womb that she has brought forth and raised all Masters upon the earth. But the attention is placed upon the Masters. She is never mentioned. It was The Great Mother called by many names of Ethiopia later called "Egypt" that brought forth greatness we refer to as males and the story was duplicated thereafter on down to the story of a Master Teacher who came by his mother Mary, a virgin. She was a Hebrew woman who bore a Hebrew child, not a Christian. It is said, God is the Father and some say The Holy Ghost. Could that have been the Great Cosmic Mother, to complete the Holy Trinity, The Father, Son and the Holy Ghost? After all, Thomas in The Book of Thomas, quotes his brother Jesus saying, "I am he who exists of the Undivided." He never announced himself as God, but he did acknowledge his mother as "The Undivided." Mary was the womb of Jesus, was of an Immaculate Conception, The Great Cosmic Mother that She is. The immaculate deception could never prove woman came from a mans rib, but still today you can go to any birthing and find a man child birthed from the loins of his mother's womb, within her rib cage. Patriarchal influence maliciously reversed the story and mans origin, and established religions that began to express superiority over women, the same concept as we have people claiming superiority over other people. Nobody is superior to any Hueman. I say, Man divided is *seeking self* but Man *undivided* is Superior. Once man Knows his origin he is secure within and of himself. Once the Human knows himself He can be Himself. Know thy Self/Heal thy Self.

All women are known for the miraculous birth of life, I call that great energy the "inner chi", Goddess, The Mother of all living" better known as the Woman or "WOMBMAN". Male and female created She them; The Undivided, The Womb of Huemanity.

It took many of life's physical experiences to call forth the answer to "WHO AM I"? From birth, given a name, number, being fed, clothed, taught to walk, talk, read, write and count to seeking man's education, integration, segregation, majors, minors, masters, then looking for a "Job", the "good Job" in order of take care of the body's wants, needs and desires for what is called "myself". But something drastically happened once there was a job. The needs were forgotten and the focus became wants and desires until debt happened. The sayings became "I'm trying.", "Trying to survive", "Trying to make a Living." Instead of seeking to "Know my Self" man learned to seek coping with stress, pain, pleasure, credit, debt, time clocks, sleep deprivation, unhealthiness, unhappiness, relationship problems, marriage, children, divorce, sickness, loneliness, not enough time, headaches, thoughts of lack and limitation, competition, striving for more and more achievements, grown children, identification, acknowledgment, compensation, reparation, discrimination, separation, and worriation. "I got to find MySelf" became a must. Before the Goddess could get anything else, she as a Maiden Goddess who expressed herself as vibrant, youthful, renewal energy in cycle after cycle of mind, body, and spirit, she had to become the full understanding of love, peace and pure energy, the great awareness of knowing herSelf.

With the desire to raise the mind in All goodness, the Goddess found her way there through the spirit of being a Mother Goddess in her creative mind and the high peak of all cycles. She is the Mother Moon and many Maiden Goddesses come to her for nurturing, advice and assistance on becoming mothers. Within the dark shadow of her own Divine Heritage is where she finds her *Self quietly sitting as a Crone Goddess, the Wise Woman whom she incorporates her energy with the Maidens and the Mothers and whom they come to for her magical formulas for healing, resolving issues and long life. She becomes the recycling Crone with the sacred pot of magic. Within her Holy chamber hidden in the womb of the treasures of darkness is the energy balance all of Huemanity is anxiously awaiting.

The Crone Goddess stretches forth her hands and arms and ascends into the ancient passage through the energetic arms of The Great Cosmic Mother, The Eternal True Beingness of Self, *(Self, being the Total Allness,) within her Divine Self.

Avivah's sky walking spirit moves upon the earth and through the many dimensions (mansions) of the Great Mother with this Mayan Cosmology purpose:

"I unify in order to influence, attracting wisdom:

I seal the process of freewill, with the magnetic tone of purpose.

I am guided by my own power doubled."

Upon discovering the Divine Self on the road to the Great Cosmic Mother, Avivah can be found on wings of the Sankofa Bird (a mythological African bird who flies forward with head turned reflecting backwards in flight, to return to the past, remembering and bringing forth past, present and future into the now forever moment of Spirit/Matter), being a catalyst for togetherness and wholeness as she glides through her own life. The egg the Sankofa bird holds in his mouth represents the Cosmic Egg of manifestation. Avivah longs to share her roadway so others who walk can notice their past and it's rippling effects to unfolding the truth of their being through experiences and telling the "story". In the comfort of knowledge that: "the earth shall be filled with knowledge" Hab. 2:14; therefore, I will not be "destroyed for the lack of knowledge" Hos.4:6. For in creating my own world, I humbly will "Be still and know that I am God" Psalm 46:10.

We either, Believe it or not.

To believe is to believe.

To know is to know is to know.

To KNOW is to own the direct personal experience that allows one to ascend into Knowing what Is. Does "Know of a surety," sound familiar? In the Bible Acts 12:11, Peter said, "Now I know of a surety ..." To assure to believe is not definite. To assure to know is.

To BELIEVE is to accept the account of what has been passed down by others through writing, which allows one to guess and wonder but not to "Know of a surety."

Truth comes to pass when being present in the moment. Two minds are not likely to occupy the same moment at the same time and have the same experience or inner knowing. It is likely that when experiencing a spiritual moment together two or more individuals will have similar and close experiences of the same truth. Knowing the Truth, guides us into each moment without doubt of what is to come because of knowing. In Knowledge sits absolute knowing. Know the *Self as gods and goddesses of the ALL. We are all agents of the Divine Energy whom some refer to as GOD i.e. Generator, Organizer, and Destroyer of all.

When one is sure about Self, then and only then can it be affirmed "I AM GODDESS of my life. I AM ONE with ALL." This is not a lesson in religion but an account of the essence of ourSelves we call "spirit".

*Wherever the word "self" is capitalized as "Self" or "SELF," even the spelling, "we," it is spelled that way in order to indicate "The Divine Cosmic Mother". That Spiritual Energy is the Divine SELF that dwells in our midst as Creation.

What's In a Name?

There is power in the names we wear throughout a lifetime, whether chosen or given. Vibration is what a name holds, either negative or positive. The energy or vibes shape and mold that person. The person called "Killer" usually is a killer. Oftentimes a person will change his or her name when they began making changes for the better, not only for spiritual energy changes about them and they began to feel different. A name will be chosen or given to refer to the nature of the person and then that name's vibration becomes what they live up to.

AVIVAH = Life, Spring, Rejuvenation, Resurrection

It is no coincidence that my mother named me Vivian, for a lively spirit, a derivative of the Italian and Spanish word "Viva", meaning "to live"! Elaine, is Greek for "Light." Avivah is a term used variously throughout the "Hueman" experience, originating from the beginning of language. It was used in the Hebrew culture and passed on as reference to a New Year beginning in the month of Aviv "Abib", known as April today. The month of April is the time of Passover. Funny that April Fool's Day falls in the month of Aviv.

In the sacred language Arabic, Avivah is pronounced Habiba.

The term "Avivah" was divinely revealed to me one morning in the early 80's. Upon awakening, I focused my eyes on a name tag I had placed on the wall the night before that read "VIVA" from Viva International Modeling Agency Inc., the name of a full figure modeling business I formed in the early 80's in uptown Atlanta. The letters "VIVA" began to literally dance and flip upon the wall of my bedroom as I laid watching the formation before my eyes, until they formed the words: "I AM." First the "I," then spaced the "A" and then the two "V's" danced and flipped to form the letter "M." By this time, I sat straight up in amazement. I later was inspired to add the letter "A" to the beginning of "Viva" and the letter "H" to the end of "VIVA," causing the word to form the "spell" "Avivah." This transformed the vibration of the letters in my spirit and a resurrecting spirit to become a constant reality for me. I Am Avivah, creating again and again. Ten years later, I learned my name is used among the nation of the Israelites. For those with the understanding of the kabalistic formulation, AHI is the sum of the alchemical vibration in the name Jehovah, YHVH. I'm saying all that to really say this: Whenever the expression "Avivah," is heard of spoken it invokes the energy of resurrection, rejuvenation and transformation.

Another quest began on the road while traveling in Israel that led my heart to one of the great geographical locations of Egypt/Kemet, another land of the Indigenous meaning black. (Egypt) is a term for "he-gypped" us of a great cultural artistry stolen and shipped it off to the British Museum." Kemet is the place of my initiation into another one of the Great Cosmic Mother's experience. There in Kemet, I laid my body in the ossuary (tomb) of one the Kings and experienced a down loaded awakening into the DNA of my own body temple of the ancient Tah Marian, (Tah=the land of, Marian=The Great Mother), One of the original Goddesses known as Isis or Hathor. These Goddesses are many, pictured and famous for The Goddess holding her son upon her lap, no doubt the first Madonna. The sacred resurgence ran through my body temple into my mental programming for my long awaited Resurrection. Mind you, I was awfully scorned by the brothers of a Hebrew sect for what I had done. I felt truly humiliated until the Head Dean of one of the Schools told them that I had done nothing wrong. They just didn't understand the importance of my moment and that I would soon come to know the purpose for the experience in the tomb.

In Ghana, originally called The Gold Coast, for its earthly deposits, I was led on a journey that seemed to be an endless quadrillion days. I was referred to as "Habiba" the reversed spelling of "Avivah", by those of the Islamic community. The letters "A" and "H" are such sacred letters because they represent the energy of breath as we breathe. "Ahhhhhhh." The letter "A" is the beginning alphabet of the English language and as Aleph is the beginning. In the Hebrew Aleph bate, the aleph "a" is silent because of it's great regenerative power alone. For there is no beginning-alpha and nor ending-omega, to LIFE.

*When the word "Hue" is used alone or with the word "man" "Hueman", it is to reference an indigenous nation of physical beings in an array of color pigmentation, aka known as melanin or melanin people. The word "human", I say, the letter "e" fell out that would indicate the idea of a people of color. Life originates in color as seen in the Rainbow.

The vibrational formula in our names is included in our "blue print" for life, so it is important to know the energy our names give out in order to know our steps on the road to our Greater Knowledge of our Greater Selves. When a Higher powered energy urges one to change or alter the name given at birth to a name that has a different energy in it, then we are honored to do so. Many times the change is for the greater work we must do to express who we truly are and to the fullest. When the name change has come, to "nic" shorten them is to demise the wealth and power of a person's royalty through the name, therefore altering the vibration of it. What we are called in life holds no impact unless we answer to that which we are called. Know ThySelf. Remember in the movie "Roots", Kunta Kinte refused to be called anything but his name.

It is of great importance to know of the health, wealth and order of the Indigenous Sovereign prior to the European's world dictatorship, then one would know of a renewal of a world sitting in a balanced orbit. The nurturing energy always prevails.

The Road to the Great Cosmic Mother is open to those who have an open mind and are not pad locked into experiences that paralyze mine expansion through opportunity to remember greatness. When consciously choosing to step on the road to the Great Cosmic Mother, fear will leave and there will be steps to guide. Although the senses may create fear, there is no harm to face. At times it appears that the road to the Great Cosmic Mother is long or an abnormal way of doing things. Some will say, "Why did it take you so long?", "What made you go that way?" or "Why did you decide to do that?" and you just don't have an answer, but you try to make up one.

Truly enough, all dead end roads are closed roads. Be careful where you choose to live. It is wise to detour from time to time until you come upon the "inner" section to The Road to The Great Cosmic Mother. The Mother's road *is* consciously that road that is less traveled. In the Little Red Riding Hood story, I often wondered why the bad wolf chose to cut off Little Red Riding Hood and eat her Grandmother, then eat her. Thank goodness there was a hunter, no doubt he was on the road himself and chose to save Red Riding Hood and her Grandmother and slew the wolf. Unless one is truly conscious of the Cosmic Mother's energy stirring in their veins, the desire to complete this journey may be weak, because there will be obstacles along the way. Only a few will even set out on the quest in the first place. Check out the stories of Harriett Tubman, the Martin Luther King and the Oprah, to name a few.

Rejuvenation, Resurrection, drives intention to assist in raising consciousness and vibrating the empowered Female energy that creates the outer balance to the male/female metamorphosis. "As we are above, so are we below."

Recently being in the presence of a King from the Ashanti tribe of Ghana, I witnessed him offer a public apology to the African descendants in America, for his ancestors, because of their selling of the people to be shipped to America. If the apology came with healing for those whose DNA was affected, that was a beautiful gift. There is something magical about apology and so that is what it takes to press or to iron out the illusion of past experiences that are not clearly remembered. Apology is a form of REPAIRation to those whose hearts were ripped and their memory lost. We spend generations every year in the remembrance of African Ancestery and without mention of the plight of the Mexican's or the Natives of America. Many of those who were dwellers of this Americas were here before any ships sailed to America. One would want to know the land that many Mothers have dwelled on for generations before claiming another. The truth is the Earth and the Fullness thereof is the Mother's Land. No one is homeless. No one is hungry. No one owns any part of the earth or its contents. There is no water shortage and that should be food for thought. That truth is the healing for forgiveness and rejuvenation. REPAIRation becomes a reality.

The Gift of Talent comes from the bloodline of strong and very powerful women, is a treasured wealth. I intend that the women in my bloodline and those I reach with innate power and talent will too recognize their Divine gifts much sooner than I have and continue to pass it on to others. Since childhood the need to express the fullness of the chalice within, forced me to pursue many various avenues of the arts. I am Self taught.

A wonderful talent passed on to me by my grandmother is a sacred art of hand craft design with fine imported cultural fabrics put on fine paper with the Goddess images that represent the Sacredness of each Female. Every movement with fine scissors in my hand was a sure knowing that Grandmother was guiding me and channeling the precision cuts in my life and to my own surprise upon my awakening the next morning, like it was Christmas to open great presents. The gift of The Goddess greeting cards are my prize expressions because of the joy they bring to my clientele and sending greetings to loved ones across the country and internationally. Among the card line are: "The Divine Goddess Collection", "Bird Brain Wisdom", "Miss Georgia Peach" and a table top photo journal of "The New Ancient Goddess". From making the cards was the inspiration to design large sizes framed ones. I began entering festival that specialized in hand crafts. The Gullah Festival is my favorite place to vend and exhibit my contributions to the museum in Buford, South Carolina.

The compilation series of art books for children brought forth a set of instructions for school teachers to teach children of all ages how to express their impressions and inner talents on paper with words and color. Story telling and art designing is what creates joy for me as well as others.

Music is also a major portion of my life being that I grew up in a musical family of singers, music instructors and pianists but chose to be the one who played by ear. Much of what I hear I don't believe anyone has ever heard it and some may not want to ever hear it again. I have found that playing on the black keys is very therapeutic as the black keys hold higher vibrations that have been withheld from hearing. Children love to play this way naturally and the sound is quite unusually intriguing. The key is to create the magic formula for healing. My new music book is "Ebony In Me". Copyright 08 avem

On the Road Again
While walking up the road to the Great Cosmic Mother's, I recall that while in a marriage and with two children, I desired to do something that was unconventional and risky business, I didn't have the support of my husband because he was not comfortable with where it might lead me. He had no idea of my steps towards my greater Self and neither did I. I stepped out on a limb that stood firm until I decided to step off. In June of 1984, Viva Full Figure International Modeling Agency was founded in uptown Atlanta, sharing inner Self esteem with hundreds of women throughout the states and strengthening myself for what was

up ahead for the Female. Becoming a consultant for major department stores was an avenue to employ many models and refer them to major magazine companies, featuring full figure models. The yearning to express my talents and show others to do the same was a must. Even my dear womb mother expressed her inner beauty, her matriarchal power, her charm and her extraordinary talents. I have become her and she me.

Through instructing enrichment courses at Emory University, "Evenings at Emory," Georgia State University and Macon Jr. College, the work was featured in a special document by a local Atlanta TV station reporter and aired on into other states around the country consulting women with a limited self esteem based on their weight and dress size. This was a service fulfilled even though I didn't have the full support of my husband. This work was not clearly accepted by him or many others because it was a designed with the concern for women of low self esteem and over the weight proportion for what is average and healthy for women.

Sacred Writings is another wonderful and revealing pastime for me. It curbs my need for conversation on the subjects that fascinate me the most and that is the plight of women, our need to know our worth and our relationships with men and the balanced harmony so very needed with them. This is the rich essence and the presence of the Great Ancestral line of Mothers as a major portion of my work on earth.

World travel and research of various cultures in many countries; Ghana, West Africa, the Gold Coast, Ethiopia, called Egypt today, Israel and other areas of Africa, also India known as the land of the Goddess Devi, Europe, Asia, and the Caribbean gave me many lives in one. My most sacred place is Ethiopia. Awakening the innate power of Goddess (Isis), Hathor and her multiple aspects of the Ultimate God is my purpose. Herstory is of the Ancient Great Matriarchal Divinity prior to man's patriarchal religious systematic conspiracy to destroy the true origin of everything even themselves, to suppress women, and not allow the power of their Divine Self expression. Experiencing my heart in Ghana, the Gold Coast, was short lived but a strong connection to the earth and the innocence of a passive yet passionate and trusting people. I was determined to return and complete that experience and I did with treasures of gift to share with others.

The Goddess warrior is present passively within every Ghanaian woman. She is busy spreading her energy through the continent patiently waiting the igniting of her greatness. These Soulful Memoires are cherished learning experiences of the universal dilemmas and that of the great endowment of The Feminine energy, through many travels. The Woman is the dormant super glue, ruling and holding for the Grand Reentrance of us into Her WOMB, once again. Huemanity is about to experience a new birth.

The road looks like a missionary's journey that lead me to passionately create an assembly for the Goddess called "G.O.D.D.E.S.S.E.E.S." The spelling of "Goddessees" is the acronym of a Sacred Truth known only among Goddesses. A Goddess who Sees knows The Truth. The ultimate goal is to rebuild the Sacred Temple within each individual who seeks it and a physical Sacred Temple on cite somewhere on the earth, for the rejuvenation of the Universal Goddess energy. Mine eye has seen the place on this planet earth. I met a group of elder women who spoke fluent English, as they invited me to sit with them in discussion of the power of the woman and they ask me what was my vision for myself and for them, I delightfully opened my secret treasure chest buried deep within my heart, of the vision I have for a sure manifestation on earth. They were amazed that this was the same vision they each had and would sit to discuss its unfolding time. I was given the approximate moment for its occurrence and was assured, the how was not my concern. I was only to show up to realize its occasion. This conversation has been repeated on many occasions throughout my travels in the most identical settings. They are U.C.M.A., The Universal Cosmic Motherhood Association. There are at least nine council women of each group.

This life is devoted to the Soul expansion of the Male/Female Energy Balance and the Goddess Power Expression. The purpose is to claim harmony with the Divine Sequence in the clock of the Cosmic Universe. Her nature, earth, air, water, Sun and Moon will know absolute respect once again. Huemanity will be totally in sync with Her cosmic clock. No one will ever say, "You're late again." while the clock is set to someone else's advantage. Her will is always on time.

Those who support religions responsible for female submission and suppression world wide, who promote drugs for healing, bombs for killing and lies for stealing have pervaded the planet and it's religions have pad locked the minds of masses from the Sacred voice of conscious Women. Love for a world without the realization of the feminine energy, as "Mother Goddess" is robbery of Self realization. One who seeks not to be one with Truth but fronts as though being for world peace is foolish. No balance, No peace. Such minds raise disobedient children to the Great Cosmic Mother with their laws of no disciplinary action towards children but children can rule and control their parents with the law. The undisciplined have ruled long enough.

Many powerful women fearlessly raise their voices, through song, writings, ministries, acting, and much more expressions of their spirit concerning the power of feminine energy and are down labeled "feminist," "nonconformists," even "militant." The Goddess is really compassionate and loving and wants for others what She wants for Herself, Divine Love. Words written in these pages are not meant to bash anyone's ethnicity nor belief, male or female. They are written to pierce the reader's eyes and ears of those who desire to set in motion a balancing order that restores the realization of peace to all and not a world by definition, label, deceit and control. In reality, life was known not too long ago of living FREE with good food, good neighbors, clothing and shelter. Now it is said, "We all have to work for a living." Do we not live to work anymore? When asked "what do you do for a living?" was anybody's answer, "I breathe for a living"? I don't think so. Some of the senses have been polluted with impurity and therefore common knowledge has flown straight out the window.

We seem to be focused on property and the possession of it, owning it, possession of people, places and things. Is Real Estate really REAL? Is it Property (possessions) that any of us must possess lawful claim to, before we return to it, to become it (dirt) once again? That's something to ponder. How can one cut out a beautiful tree and sell it for a Christmas decoration then three days later throw it back to the ones still living. How cruel is that? As indigenous beings to the earth, we were to be stewards of the earth and protect the land from robbers and rapists. It is most of our experiences to know what it is to be chattel to someone and even to the powers that be.

One who opposes to eradicate their comfort of such captivity is already captivated, oppressed and in bondage with fear beyond return. They are one with it, only to be ripped from it, by the Noble force of Nature, the Power that **IS**. This is the emergence that rushes me to complete my journey on "The Road to the Great Cosmic Mother."

This work gives credit to the ancestors who speak and write through me to express what is in the here and now for me through my walk on this road of an awakening journey.

Any quotes made are purely to express once again Truth, not to discredit anyone. I acknowledge with great respect, all great writers past, present and future.

The names and titles in the memoirs are purely fictitious and any indication to any one known today is truly spiritual and with permission.

Introduction to the Memoirs and Stories

The Love of my being longs to reach out to the universe and back. My heart's pump is as strong as The Great Cosmic Mother whose will is to make her presence known upon the earth in these final days before restoration. I seek those who seek transformation by the renewal of our minds. To know the absolute is to pervade illusion. The stories are to tell of situations that can come of our paths to give us the opportunities to expand our horizons and break taboos. The stories also assist in stretching the imagination of the events that may be possible to create "the way" on the road to the Greater Self. The memoirs are the accounts that brought closer encounters with the True kind for a detachment of the Hueman experience and surrender to the Divine will of Manifestation.

The Road to The Great Cosmic Mother is a Journey of Memoirs and Stories that lead to the life I know not of until I arrive. It may sometimes appear that I travel it all alone but I remember to focus on that great ancestral flood light within the guide. My ancestors walk with me, through me and as me with their still soft inner voice saying: "Still yourself child, and know the Power that I AM is within you and that you are within I AM."

The walk through life can appear so many ways. The road can be merry or it can be challenging, up and down those hills unknown as to what is up ahead but I never walk along. No need to fear the dark for She walks with me, in me, as me.

I must admit that my willingness to produce this creative writing is inspired and the Great and Divine Mothers who are the SKYWALKERS of my soul and the Omnipresent Master Mind within are the Visioneers having their visions expressed through those whose desire is to recall that Divine Original Power.

The Road to The Great Cosmic Mother are memoirs and stories of traumatic and extraordinary situations that lead to the moment I realized the Power of knowing what it means to really be a Goddess and the strength of making a difference to other women seeking the ultimate empowerment of being the "Womb of men," as the Holy Bible states "The Mother of All Living." There is what I call the "ego" simply ourSelves acting like we don't know who we really are. It is a great revelation to know what is real is reflected by our senses and that upon knowing my true self, what the senses report, the true Self magnifies unthinkable. I am glad I have that much sense. It is in detaching from the desire to be right about everything, that I am coming to know mySelf. I AM That I AM.

I do not write to have anyone believe what is true for me. I write to put out what is on my mind, and create a vacuum for more ideas. This is my joy. This writing is of creative expression and reflection.

Becoming more and more conscious of thought, what I say and what I do assists me in knowing if it is the action of my soul or me acting like I don't know who I am.

I became clear when my teacher Roy Eugene Davis suggested I pray *in* God *in* mySelf vs. pray *to* God external *to* mySelf." Praying *in* God is praying *in* your Divine Self. Praying *to* God is like praying or taking the person next door or "the man upstairs." Not sure if the prayer has been answered or not, by something or somebody external to yourSelf. Meditation is the direct path to the Divine Self.

Right and wrong are judgments of not knowing or acting like judgment will make a difference. The nature of not knowing seeks to rule and regulate and to debate and argue to stay alive and energized. I attempted to draw the ego and all I could come up with was a big potato head falling way back, with a huge grin, two beady eyes, with long stick arms and legs.

Being a left handed artist, I desired to see what the world was like from all angles, illusionary and real. I was a "day dreamer" in school and a wonderer of just what I was learning was going to be of any beneficial value to me or to anyone else. In my adult life, I ran across an old high school teacher of mind and I reminded him that when I sat it his class of world history, his was the best subject because I was able to use my creative visual eyes. I told Mr. Woods that in his class while he taught, I pictured myself in those places in my mind. Then later in my adult years I literally visited most of those places in my body. He was amazed, then he laughed and said that he had never left the states, he lived in them, went to school in them only to teach about the world from a text book. "How about that?" he said. I was delighted that he took my number and invited to come to his class to give a talk on my travels. He served me with a great vision and I was able to serve it back to those who had a great creative imagination to do the same.

What appears cloudy or unclear is simply a dim illusionary perception to what really is, until we see clearer with a more realistic purpose. It only takes intending to see clearly the truth about the matter and what life is showing you. Life is always giving out opportunities that really are wonder full. What appears perfect reflects the truth about who I am and the same with what appears to be imperfect.

Walking up the road to the Great Cosmic Mother, I found a stream of wisdom, that I am the Master Rower of the boat. I have had to row when there seemed to be a struggle with strong turbulence. God, in me, as me, handled it, without a paddle. Peace begin to shows up when I lean back, realizing I have done all that you can do and watch each pebble as I walk on through and go with the flow of the stream. That is when the situation clears up. "Take your hands off of it" the old folks would say.

I'll take nothing for the experiences on my life journey. I could see where I was headed once I had come so far and saw how I got through so many situations.

Nothing exists outside of me except what I gave attention to as though it is real. Knowing who I am allows me to see the eternal thread that binds "us" into oneness. I am the creator of what seems to go against me and the unique creations that bring my attention back to oneness. I now keep my focus on that which is real. What is real is You and Me. That which I can see is a reality. Spirit is seen when it becomes flesh. Thanks Rabiah, it is true that the easiest way to hide the woman was to make her a Holy Ghost, The Father, Son and Holy Ghost. The invisible woman was also referred to as "wisdom", given to Solomon.

It is the greatest revelation to realize that when I step away from the path, I don't have to beat myself up or allow any one do it for me. I just step right back on again and keep going. That is part of the Divine Order of life. Eventually I will get where I intend to be. I didn't always get to the finish line right away or in seven days. I just got there when I did. My seven days could be eleven days or two. I had to realize that to finish is to complete and began again and sometimes beginning brings over what was left at the finish line when there is desire to review for improvement. So I've stopped fussing and started going with the flow of life.

When I am clear and conscious each and every moment, I can't trick myself with upsets. Love is too powerful. I love to write and talk about Love, because I am and Love just turns me on.

It is my The Great Cosmic Mothering self who is the mover of this automobile (the body) that glides throughout life's provided experiences, while lovingly abiding and guiding Her will. Breathing becomes natural and healing unnecessary to a perfect and divine life.

My memoirs and stories are mine to share that we have them but we are not them. They are simply records of the past, present and future rolled up into one auspicious moment.

Being awake to the moment, memoirs and stories cease to exist. I breathed a new experience. I have taken notice that when my experiences are joyful. It is then that I speak less of needs and wants and become content in the moment. It is then two roads began to merge into one.

Even roads to perdition … lead to the road to The Great Cosmic Mother. Don't try to figure out what part of my writing is not about The Great Cosmic Mother. It's All Her.

What is attracted to our moments is a reflection of what and how we view ourselves and where we are in consciousness and is a measuring gage of the cosmic mileage we travel. When we are clear of our desires in life, and give up our attachments to life, life just shows up so fulfilling and delightful. Life begins to take on the appearance of what we become and our surroundings naturally blend into us as a whole.

In life, I always desired what it must be like to be a Princess, a Queen, a Goddess, and Noble woman in the world, doing what will one day make a huge difference to huemanity, the earth, the universe and the entire cosmos. I really didn't know what that looked like and I don't know that any does prior to becoming such. It just happens based on intention, action, focus and will.

As I continue on in my walk, I changed more shoes than I did hats. From booties to sneakers and right away to boots and now I can skate my way into the next moment with ease. Simpler, I become that which I call forth by my very desire and thoughts and it brought me a degree of peace about myself. It also brought out the purpose of my being here at this moment in time, in spite of the web that holds the "Hue man" fiber. I let go and allow what is to be.

I must share with you of the next curve on the road to mySelf, people, nature and all began to be in harmony with "me". Pain, mind, body and soulful pain began to diminish from my life. I certainly didn't agree with it but there again the cosmic measuring rod of consciousness would set up a test of pain that I would have the opportunity once again to step into the "Heal Thy Self" class. The bumps and bruises may be there but they are not permanently. Understanding the meaning of pain and knowing how to remove it replaces attention on the Road to The Great Cosmic Mother and the purpose for life. I have noticed that when I am being, doing and having what I love, I feel good. I become the present.

In the memoirs, "Seeing Double" and "The Garden of Eve" are mountains standing tall in the sea of life that once climbed to the top of them, a beautiful TRUTH appeared. Religion, mis-education, politics, economic theories, etc.,

etc., etc. appears clearly to be what they truly are, illusions. That can be someone else's reality.

Life is becoming a "hands off" experience that reveals mySelf allowing the order of peace that is naturally a part of life. It is like suddenly realizing when traveling in your automobile you have gone a distance and then it seems you were not there for a few miles back and you wonder how you were driving if you paid no attention to the road and yet you have safely come a ways regardless. Where was I? and who was navigating the automobile. That was a "hands off" moment when it was really the SELF operating.

"Love isms"

I came to Love mySelf in a way, that I could see how I was once trapped in the affection of an illusionary love. I was totally infatuated with luvvv. The way I was being with myself and with others was literally unreal.

In my dark days of illusion, pretending I didn't know who I was, I thought someone had to bring love to me. I didn't remember that a mate was the reflection of the love I already was. So when I didn't feel love, I thought something was wrong with him. It was the Love that I AM that I attempted to be blind of, to trade off for Luvvv. We both waited for the Love to show up while being unhappy in Luv with one another. I didn't remember true Love was unconditional and that the individual package covering was not the necessary main focus. I thought what I viewed on TV was relationship love but it was not genuine, it was TV luvvv. Wow I began to miss the sister, mother and grandmother kind of love. Now there is another kind my family didn't tell me of? There is Divine Love, Divine Marriage, and Divine Sex. That is The Creation of the Divine Family. People often hurt because of living lies in the name of luv, never forgiving grudges that keep them all blown up as though they just want to explode and let it all out. Let go of the fake Luvvv and just be for Real. It feels so much better.

Too many songs were written about this kind of love. Yet we all wanted to be in it. One song that I question the writer is "If loving you is wrong, I don't want to do right" When did Love ever become wrong? What kind of love is that? Now I know. I wrote a song to say: "If loving you is wrong, why don't we make this thing right." I don't mean to sound like a love bug flower child, but actually Pure Love is the glue that brings all things together. What is *pure* love? Here I go again. It's the kind of love that you just don't expect anything from the other, you just want to give it because it feels good to you. Like, "I Love *you*, and we don't have to do anything about it," kind of love. Of course, love has to be received the same way.... unconditionally.

Family, relationships, work, career, goals, health, wealth—everything that has to do with living is based on how much love I am operating with. Money is another energy but not greater than Love. Someone once said, money is somewhere up there close to oxygen. I hear women say, "I don't need a man." I say, "You're right, we just ought to want one, to share the love we already have." I don't want just a man, because there are many expressions of a "man." I am specific of the man I choose to express mySelf with. He is not to complete me but the two of us completed can enhance the wholeness that we are together. Some walk around wondering what is wrong, "why am I not meeting that right man?" Everyone I meet is the one that is my reflection. So he is the right one for that moment. Until I say "Oh no he's not." I go check in the mirror of my Great Self and make the adjustments and then say "next". It is the mirror that tells me what to change so that the whole ensemble will come together. I have to remember that I AM never alone but when two becomes one the energy multiplies. Oh, I love to dance alone sometimes and it is also hot when those other arms catch hold of my waist as I feel energy blend up as one. We become a whirlwind, then a tornado. Look out!

Love becomes luvvv when it gets icky and sticky with conditional contracts and expectations, prenuptials, rules and regulation. Real Love just IS. When I simply agree with him to disagree peacefully, peace will prevail. Real Love, Pure Love has no "Sick-ness".

Nothing is more beautiful as to see a mother-to-be awaiting her "birthday" the day she gives birth to the "earthday" of her baby, a brand new gift of Love. Love turns sour and becomes Luvvv, from conditioning and training and the expectations of the world that comes with it. Then I fall. I fall in luv. In Pure Love I Rise.

Who teaches the newborn that upon entering a new realm of life they are to remember their purpose for coming on the scene? We often carry out their purpose to the maximum and not get caught up in the illusionary conversation of lack, limitation, fear, worry, and separation from that which IS REAL.

As soon as I can place one foot in front of the other and proceed to take seven steps alone, I have walked into the living room of falsehood. A world already made up with false ideas for controlling the masses. Why am I not then given back to the Great Cosmic Mother in a ceremony that will impact me as the baby as much as the hospital trauma? Love is traded for Luv. Just as Kunta Kinte was offered up to the Most High Creator in the movie "Roots" I too must remember to bless my gifts at birth and give thanks for what I have the opportunity to give and receive through others.

I keep this remembrance of what "The Prophet Kahlil Gibran" said about love. "When Love comes to you follow him, though his ways are hard and steep. And when his wings enfold you, yield to him, though the sword hidden among his pinions may wound you. And when he speaks to you believe in him, though his voice may shatter your dreams as the north wind lays waste the garden. For even as love crowns you so shall he crucify you. Even as he is for your growth so is he for your pruning. Even as he ascends to your height and caresses your most tender branches that quiver in the sun, so shall he descend to your roots and shake them in their clinging to the earth. Like sheaves of corn, he gathers you unto himself. He threshes you to make you naked. He sifts you to free you from your husks. He grinds you to whiteness. He kneads you until you are pliant; and then he assigns you to his sacred fire that you may become sacred bread for God's sacred feast. All these things shall love do unto you that you may know the secrets of your heart and in that knowledge become a fragment of Life's heart. But if in your fear you would seek only love's peace and love's pleasure, then it is better for you that you cover your nakedness and pass out of love's threshing-floor, Into the seasonless world where you shall laugh, but not all of your laughter, and weep, but not all of your tears. Love gives naught but itself and takes naught but from itself. Love possesses not nor would it be possessed, for love is sufficient unto love. When you love you should not say, "God is in my heart," but rather, "I am in the heart of God." And think not you can direct the course of love, for love, if it finds you worthy, directs your course. Love has no other desire but to fulfill itself. But if you love and must have desires, let these be your desires: to melt and be like a running brook that sings its melody to the night, to know the pain of too much tenderness, to be wounded by your own understanding of love, and to bleed willingly and joyfully, to wake at dawn with a winged heart and give thanks for another day of loving, to rest at the noon hour and meditate love's ecstasy, to return home at eventide with gratitude; and then to sleep with a prayer for the beloved in your heart and a song of praise upon your lips." This is the writing of the Prophet Kahlil Gibran.

Being turned on and tuned in to TV, radio, news paper, miseducation, malls, sports competitions, fashion, culture, politics and religion creates the misunderstanding of sex, wealth, health, and true love. There is a serious distortion of Divine consciousness due to the focus on the external world.

There is no need to seek Love because Love is what I am anyway. Love can't be lost or found. It is the electricity that is always in place when plugged in to it.

Being in and of Pure Absolute Divine Love relationships, takes on a higher vibration in expression. There is no such thing as making love and broken love or love sickness, not even blindness. This thinking creates an erroneous distorted form of CON-troll and manipulated games. Live in the moment and Love shows up.

Finding what I thought was lost, was just some place else is such a relief. Where there is fun, laughter, and joy, there is no pain unless you laugh until it hurts. Where there is pain, joy soon follows. Where there is play, there is no aging. Where there is no aging, there must be fun. I make everyday my earthday celebration.

In the days of this writing, I was coming into a greater knowledge of mySELF. I can say that, that which was needed to fine tune myself began to show up all around me. I found that I couldn't resist observing mySELF and I had to allow those I knew that loved themselves truly to call me on my ignorance and support me in moving to another level of Love.

There wasn't the slightest resistance and this revealed that the time had come to become correct in my Greatness. I was being transformed by the renewing of my mind to oneness with my God mind. I was accepting a new mind. Renewal can come by pain of changing from what had become comfortable. Like finally throwing away that old comfortable pair of shoes for to break in a new pair was going to hurt a little. Then they get comfortable until time for another new pair. Then growing out of the old into the new becomes easy.

I heard of the most impactful, evolving, experience when I met a man that told me he had suffered so much pain in his back constantly throughout his life. He said that when he was a young boy his mother would take him to the cotton field with her to pick cotton for the owner of the plantation and his back began to hurt so bad he had to stop for rest. When the cotton field owner came by he ordered him to get up very meanly and get back to work. He knelt once again in severe pain and this time his own mother sharply scolded him to get up and he told her that his back was hurting too bad to go on. She slapped him and told him, "You have no back!" He was 11 years young then. Today as he was speaking to me while getting physical therapy treatment at age 65, he spoke of a recent day when he was feeling a lot better until he and his wife had a serious disagreement and in their heated moment of exchanging insults, she shouted out to him as he was descending their stairs, "You don't have a back bone in your body." He said his back went out with the worst pain that threw him back to the first time of hearing those similar words from his first love, his mother, now from his wife. I have recognized such upsets and setbacks from past moments of conditional love.

All along my road, I met my matches of who I was being at the time. You ever heard your mama tell you "alright now, you gonna meet your match someday."

Meaning, somebody just like you or return to you what you give out to somebody else. When I didn't like what kept coming up, I just had to make an adjustment to who I was being at the time. So, instead of being mad at what showed up in life for myself, I had to change myself and be mySELF, for REAL.

"It is better to express than to impress."

Speaking on talents of the SELF, as I grow in Absolute Divine Intelligence, I evolve into different areas of expressions even to the point of creating a social structure that works for me. I can be in it truly and not be with it, even though it appears to be all around me. I sometimes out grow my relationships and when there is a sense of disharmony, I would simply ask to experience life without resistance to Divine Will. When having discovered my talents within mySELF, I sought to use then and when I didn't use them, I noticed they would get away from me or go dormant. It is like the talents show up when we do and leave when we do. My talents make the impression when I express mySELF.

After approaching the light of The Great Cosmic Mother, there was a great change in ideas. I attracted those who had always been with me. I sometimes chose to be creative in dress, hair, expression, and food intake. I sometimes chose to make a change in associations. I put on a new me. By this, I mean with a change in view of mySelf for who I really am, my choice of relationships to people shifted to those who speak the "same language" or on the same page.

Changing names, titles, and ideas and going so far as to changing residence, city, state, and country, is a sign of growth. I love change. Change allows me to know more of mySelf. When it became uncomfortable to those who had been around me and didn't really KNOW me, I knew it was the new Light bulb that came on that sometimes is blinding and creates discomfort to those who saw me in a different light. It's like putting in bug lights that chases the bugs away.

Talents are my way of being somewhere else in many expressions of mySelf.

When I experience events that appear shocking and painful, I don't hesitate to re-member mySELF or to know mySELF. I call out loudly, "Where are you Mamuuuu! And quickly in my tiresome climb up that road, Mother shows up as MySelf to the rescue. Girrrrrrrrl. I sigh out release fully. To know is great; to know that you know is even greater.

With this awareness, I began to move into a place where sharing with others is the opportunity to "Be" mySELF. This became the focus of my travel up the road to the Palace of The Great Cosmic Mother. That is what I came to do and I love doing just that. Again, my purpose in life is to unify in order to influence, attracting wisdom, sealing the process of freewill with the magnetic tone of purpose. I am guided by my own power doubled. With this knowledge of my own divine purpose for living, in my walk there may still be pebbles on the road or boulders, but wisdom will lead me on.

Yes, all will eventually arrive to The Great Cosmic Mother's arms in their inner knowing and know the moment of arrival.

Introduction to the story of
SEEING DOUBLE

I say that when there are so many holes in my life, that in order for me to stay in the moment, I choose to patch those holes up, and to be at peace.

The holes were obstacles that tore into my life at early ages are a couple that I will mention and say how I dealt with them. The first remembrance is at age 10 months, when my mother took me to be christened (a sophisticated way of being baptized) at the neighborhood Church one Sunday morning. When being sprinkled upon my forehead, I recall being somewhat skeptical about the whole ordeal. Yes, at the age of 10 months. I know that is why the drama is as real to me as of this day. Mother told me that as the minister sprinkled my forehead, I let out a scream that sounded like a four letter word beginning with the letter "S" and ending with the letter "T."

I could not believe a baby would know such a word, but I do remember a flash forward scene of the minister harming me in some way in some time to come. When I turned 9, that following November, when the neighbors were shopping for Thanksgiving, my mother sent me to the neighborhood grocery store to get vanilla flavor for baking. As I walked past the "Reverend's" house, (i.e. the one who sprinkled me when I was 10 months old) he called me to the side door, asked me to come in and to bring him something from the store. He pulled my little chubby self up on his lap as he counted out change from the table covered with change, no doubt, from the collection plate. He then seized the moment to ram his filthy finger into my vagina. When I let out a scream and violently scurried to get off of his lap, he covered my mouth and tightened his other arm around my waist, then scolded me in my ear saying "You better not tell anything, little girl about this or Santa Claus will never come to see you again, you here me?" He let me down, I kicked him as hard as I could and ran as fast as I could, all while I felt very uncomfortable in my private area.

Where I ran, I don't remember, I probably ran home to my sacred chamber in the corner of the closet of our front room. This is where I could go to talk to those ancestors that always, always were there to listen to me when I could tell no one what was going on in my world. I knew I could never tell anyone about this experience. Christmas was the worst day of my life from then on. I remember in that moment, I had my little life flash backwards to that day when I was christened by this monster. I experienced my first "déjà vu." This was a tragedy to me, because I felt I had to keep this confidential, as much as I was very expressive. I was abused by someone who was an "outstanding figure in the community," was what an adult neighbor said to my mother once. I was perplexed over this for a long time. I believe that my grandmother suspected something was wrong with me but I was good at not giving her anything to worry about. "Grandma" was my girl. I let her be gone from my life before I allowed this to come out.

I was 21 in my second year of a 24 year marriage before I finally released it. My husband then was a support to me and wanted to kill this man, but he was already passed on, so lucky for him and my husband. Later I found out I was not the only one he had hurt that way. For my own Self, I know that it was not a tragedy but an experience that gave me a story to share with others that we are put at the cross roads again to choose whether to be a victim of the circumstance or a volunteer to share the experience to others that they have the same choice. "Do not let your circumstances cripple your life." Some how The Great Cosmic Mother took care of that situation because I didn't remember it again until years after I had worked at a Rape Crisis Center. I heard myself share the situation with other molested and rape victims. My sharing allowed them the choice of allowing this to be something that kept them frozen or move on. After all, no one can take what you don't give away. Not your self-respect, nor your femininity.

Another devastating event "came to pass." At age 12, a man, whom my mom and auntie said was my dad drove to Georgia from California with another man. They came and visited for 15 minutes, it seemed. I saw my mother pass him a $1.00 bill behind my back which he gave me to go and buy an ice cream cone and then I disappeared. I was puzzled by that action of my mother doing that but latter in life a friend thought that she might have wanted to send me away for a few minutes. That was a better thought. I never saw that man again in life. My father, I was told died, somewhere in my adult age. So in growing up, the neighbors rumored that the Jew man who owned the neighborhood grocery store around the corner was my dad. Growing up, I wondered why they thought that. I had no idea who my dad was. I was told that my mother went to California at her age of 21 to help with her mother's elder sister, who needed some assistance in her old age, and mother met a man who was 10 years older and they became friends. Mother was pregnant with her first child, i.e. me, married him or vice versa and when my Grandmother found out she had Mama leave the man and return home. Thank goodness she allowed me to come too. Obviously, there was a great purpose for me to be here now.

Mother's brother played a very important role as a male figure in my life, because he loved the women in our family, worked two jobs and financially supported his mom, my mom and my two sisters who came five years apart after me. I love them dearly. There were tons of family secret in the closets, you dared peep into, but I created a technique for my own unsolved mysteries. I call it "The Final Touch". It is like completing an unfinished sentence or an unfinished painting. Being an artist, I began to paint the rest of my experience with a story that is realistic fiction. It was like turning out the light when every body has gone, and making sure there is no one to trip in the dark. Meaning all other characters are definitely fictitious. The outcome from start to finish completely solves the mystery and gives peace at the same time. I could stand back and say, "Well that finishes that, I brush my hands off and go on." The illusion of pain, anger and sorrow is gone for good. The unsolved mystery is an illusion and so is the finished touch. It becomes the preferred ending of a story you would have had it to be. No one likes waking up from an unfinished dream or a nightmare. In "Seeing Double," I will have the "Final Touch" of Sondra's family saga with a creative solved, realistic yet fiction mystery. This allowed for crossing the road of great pot holes and continuing on to The Road to The Great Cosmic Mother.

Since seeking out others to give answers to issues, I came to know that it is through myself that I solve the issues at hand, merely because they are only illusions indicating that within the "problem," resides the solution. The question always compels the answer. We as women in particular are "Problem Solvers." In resurrecting the mother wit, the intuitive wise mother within that Knows all, sees all, and is all; when telling ourselves "We can't know everything" ceases and when becoming The Goddess we are meant to be, will be when we come to know just who the mystery solver really is.

"Seeing Double" is one of the challenges that seemed to take half a life time to put the final touch on. No challenge comes without the opportunity to master it.

Sandra was born into a situation where she did not get to know the man her mother was with at the event of her conception. As in the early most ancient days of women history, a mother's brother, if she had one either older or younger, was most responsible to a family where the father figure was gone, was spiritually assigned to be the guardian over his mother and his sister's children. He did a great job. Her Grandmother was "the head Mama," Mama was Mama and Auntie was another form of Mama as well. That was the village that took care of the family. We become very clear as to why we have the experiences we do. Sandra's uncle provided in particular the upper middle class of high cultured life style, such as classical music, fine art, the finest in clothing, even to learn to play musical instruments such as the clarinet and the piano. On Sundays after a big dinner of 12 or more family and friends at the table, we held a family musical concert in the living room.

Still longing for the person that all the kids called "daddy," but one she could call her own. What is the real role of a "daddy" except to contribute the best way he can. The "daddy" role is a very easy one really. Mothers have the total responsibility of the internal life, the birthing, nurturing, and rearing to the age that the child becomes aware of the Self.

In many a family, I am sure that there was someone that the family told was a brother but turned out to be a cousin or the person thought to be your Mama was really your Auntie. The closet was full of skeletons and you could very well have been one of them.

So, with my talent for creative writing and creative visualization, not having the whole picture, I grew up and finished the picture of my self and sold the work of art to "L.I.F.E." i.e. "Life Is For the Enlightened." "L.I.F.E." became the title of a workshop/seminar that my participants successfully got free of their unsolved mysteries through story telling and creative realistic fiction writing.

The truth is, no matter what situation we are "born" into or at any point in life we find our Self, through what seems like something that needs fixing, we will have the direct opportunity to work on it only to become aware of the Truth, that everything is perfect just the way it is. Nothing is broken, we just choose to spend our lifetime fixing it.

The story of SEEING DOUBLE

We all have heard the expression or even spoke it ... "My, you sure do look like someone I've seen before. You got a twin somewhere?" Not only that, we all have experienced directly or at least indirectly, the findings of family skeletons in places never imagined to turn up. Like I stated, tares and holes in my life sometimes had to be mended in order me to move on to the next life experience. There is no need to stress out when you can go with the flow or create a way through it that only has effects on your life story. Life unfolds in the most shocking ways sometimes, and when we clear our minds from the shock of it, we can rise to rewarding heights.

"Who Am I?"

Here I am in my early 40's preparing to exhibit my art work outside of the US. The exhibit scheduled to take place in the next few weeks. I had showings of my work in quite a few galleries in the states, which are doing just fine with the help of a great staff. Even with that, there is so much to be done in getting prepared to travel abroad and setting up business in another country. It is so hot here in Florida this July, I find it hard to leave the house. Being so busy, I decided to ride out and spend some time with my mother. I knew she loved fresh fruit, so I stopped to get her some fresh peaches and mangos. Mama and I are very close and can talk about almost anything except my father and why I never knew him. I had the chance to do some deep thinking, while driving to her home. The only thing I've ever known her to do was raise flowers and plants for her florist business, which is doing very well but she still seems to be missing being in love. There is not one man in her life or anyone else for that matter, except for her house assistant Lilly and her sister Clara, who lives up north in New York. Oh and a long lost friend she rarely mentions unless I bring her up. She lives somewhere in California. Mama is quiet about a few things.

My Auntie Clara says Mama has been that way since she left California with me as an infant, but I too have practically been a loner and when finding the time to have an affair, it didn't last long because my career was my first priority. For the most part, I am pretty much at ease with my business. Well, I should say that the time that I am not, I get pretty intense with curiosity of my past. The fact of not knowing was driving me crazy.

It's 12 o'clock noon in Egypt and I needed to stop and call about the Grand Opening of the art gallery over there. "Hello, this is Sondra More; may I speak with Mohammed please!" Ha, I am shouting as though they can't hear me across the water on the telephone. "Mohammed? Yes, I am fine. How are things coming?" I could hear a delay in our speaking and it did sound far away. "Great! Oh excuse me, you did what! You said you just sold my most expensive piece!? Which was? Nooooo! Not that one! No, no, no. That was the painting of my mother! There was a pause, "Mohammed, are you there? Can you hear me? Okay, Mohammed, that piece was not for sale, I sent it only for sentimental reasons and to hang in the gallery as just an attraction. It is my good luck piece. Oh, you do not understand. It is not for sale! Mohammed! The "not for sale" note must have fallen off somehow! That was the original! You must get it back, right away! Do you understand Mohammed?"

He answered to my shouting, "Yes Madam, I do understand now. Someone traveling from California has purchased it, Madam Sondra. I am so sorry. I, I, will try, I will see what I can do to trace him." I heard my own echo repeating to myself ... Someone traveling from California has purchased it; someone from Kerrington, California. "Did you say Kerrington?" "Yes." That is the upscale town where I was so secretly born. Who from Kerrington would be in Egypt and purchase my American painting, then take it all the way back to Kerrington? A painting of my mother at that! That is so unimaginable! My insane reason for sending it there was because mama had once made the comment that, the only way she'd ever leave America would be in a flower box. She even made me agree to bury her in a pine box with flower petals from her 5 acre botanical garden, all around her, showing her face only, or in one of my picture frames, as a picture only. She said this laughing, although I knew she meant it. I knew she was afraid of flying although she would consider a cruise.

With all of that, I decided to paint a very fine oil portrait of mama, last summer, wearing a very wide brim straw hat with all the flowers she grew, on the brim. I will admit that it is the most beautiful piece I'd ever done. I got pretty generous offers for it too, so I made several prints of it. I thought the original I would never part with.

This portrait took a lot of patience sitting with her and quality time as well. I told her jokingly, yet seriously, that when I went to Egypt, she would travel with me, and I did just that.

It is true; you have to be careful what you think and what you say, because it will materialize. Now I'm hearing that it has been sold to someone traveling to California. "Who on earth is the buyer Mohammed?" I was shouting this time with panic to myself.

Although, I was not angry, he felt a sudden reaction of anxiety to get the portrait back. "Please, do what you have to, to get it back. Mohammed, I'm not worried, I know you will take care of it for me. I will call tomorrow." When I hung up the phone, I began to ponder the coincident that someone would be interested in that particular painting and of all places, Egypt, and take it, of all places, to Kerrington Heights, California, the small city I was born in. Well, it is just a painting of my mom. I still have her and she did get to Egypt, after all, and may be headed back to Kerrington. She must have some unfinished business there too, I thought. Or maybe I do. Oh, I have enough abstract going on in my life, so why paint another picture of more. Not to worry though. Who ever got it, if it's meant for them to have it, they will. On the other hand, if it's for me to get it back, I will. It's totally priceless.

"Now She Tells Me."

I hurried back to my car and continued on to moms place, and reached her about 45 minutes later. Just before I got to the entrance of her villa, a thought came to me that I should contact Auntie Clara and see her on my flight change on Friday. There are some things that are cropping up in my life that I need to clear up once and for all. I'm sure she of all people can help enough. I want to know this man before he dies, if it is not too late.

As soon as I pulled up, she walked out of the green house to greet me. "Hi Mama"! I yelled out. "Come on in Sandra." "Mom your flower garden is so beautiful I could see it a mile away, driving in. Your florist business is flourishing very well?" "Yes it is baby." "Oh, here I brought your favorite fruit from the market, Mom." "Thank you dear, you shouldn't have, but I'm glad you did." She bent over and kissed me on my fore head with one of her cute little giggles, as I lay sprawled out on my favorite lounge chair. I set up to tell her that I was leaving on Friday to get to Egypt and wanted to stop by to make sure she was all right.

She assured me she was all right and that I shouldn't worry about her. "What about yourself, are you all right, you stay so busy with your art work and all." "You know that in my line of work I never have to leave here at all Sondra." "Well Ma, I think you can show a little love for yourself and take time out for a cruise or something." "You know, I was thinking of doing just that. Maybe you can go with me." "No, you should go alone and meet some other interesting people like yourself. You just go right ahead Mama and have some fun I'll be just fine, I am looking forward to the Grand Opening of my North East African Museum. Who knows what the future holds for us anyway. I say just keep on living and doing what you love to do and the best is yet to come."

Mom was looking very bleak and complex about something, so I allowed her to just be still for a moment. I had to break her silence; it was a bit intense. "Mom, Mom, what is it?" She turned away with tears in her eyes and began to walk out to the garden. Following her I asked, "What's on your mind?" She sat down on the soft cushioned chair and as I watched her take a deep breath, I knew I was about to hear something earth shaking and revealing. "Sondra, sit down." Now I'm, sure. "I am sitting mother, what is it?"

"I am about to tell you something that has been choking me alive for too long, like all of your life." All of my life; I braced myself. "I have reaped the consequences of withholding it from you." I just listened intensely. "It's about your birth." Oh, I felt a rush from my toes to my head in a split second. Woman, Will you spit it out! I thought. "When you were born Sondra, there was also another baby." "What do you mean, I had a twin?" "Yes." "What happened to the twin, Mother? "I lost her at birth." Now there really was intense silence and then I wanted to scream that I was just hearing this, but I have always known somehow. I took a long deep breath through my nostrils, to preserve my energy and keep my peaceful spirit in tact. Calmly I responded not to loose any more information from her. "Yes Mother, I am listening." I was beginning to stand up in speaking to her but I decided to remain seated and thinking, what to do with this information at this late date. She slowed down. "I am now in my mid 40's and you are yet to tell me anything about my father. Are you now ready to tell me about him?" "I was forced to leave him, Sondra."

"What do you mean you were forced to leave him?" She got up and began to walk swiftly out of the room and through the house. The ranch house was so large I was not about to chase after her for any more words. To hold on to the past is like being glued to a chair for the rest of your life.

"Mother you have to stop running off and not telling me the complete truth that is tormenting you! I refuse to allow your past to stop me from moving forward!" I screamed out to her. "I have not spent half of my life waiting for you to now tell me half of the truth. Why not get over your misery and tell the whole truth!" I had reached her bedroom where she was crying her eyes out into her pillow. "God, what is it!"

I got conscious that she might become very ill. I sat down beside her on the bed and just stared into space. In a calm voice, "I have been so desiring to know a side of myself that is a mystery to me and you know the whole truth, but you give me a large portion and yet, you still whole back a very important part from me that could possibly be a breakthrough for me and you. Well, you know what Mother? I am *not* going to pick any more of the truth from you that I think will make me free. I now know that I have to find the rest of the truth for myself. I will do that for myself. You have been so selfish with your life. I allowed that to cause an effect on mine, but as of today, I take full responsibility for the rest of my life. This is a good day Mother!" I had had it with her by now. "You can stop crying, you've manipulated me with your crying tantrums to not tell me any more than you wanted me to know. It's okay Mother! I will be just fine. I just have to say this to you this way, because I am tired of the pain, the search, and the unknown part of me that I've been dragging around with me in my net of life, weighing me down. It affected me more than you know. The biggest part has been in my relationships toward men, that imbalanced portion of myself that keeps me in and out of relationships and not being truthful with them and most of all my relationship with myself, whom I am not sure who that is. Right about now, I'm going to know for sure. I realize in this moment that I have to let this go and move on. I forgive you, I forgive my father, and I forgive myself!"

I called forth the balanced male/female energy to be complete with the absence of and the feeling of inadequacy for not knowing my biological father. "Mom, I'm giving you one more shot, for the love of God, release the truth about the past concerning me and live a healthy life! Will you do that please?"

I stood again, but this time I was ready to just walk out even if I never saw her again. As I returned to my senses, I really did begin forgiving. The pain seemed to run out of the door in front of me and I felt tired.

I will get the closure I need. I walked as fast as she ran behind me shouting something about not being able to stay with my father and having to leave. I didn't want to hear any more. I just got in my car and drove away as fast as I could, in attempt to put this as far behind as possible. I wanted to finalize this and hoped she and I could come to some completion that we both could move on in life. Where I was in my spiritual growth, I began to see that this was the healing I have been longing so all my life.

Calmness fell over me all of a sudden, as I was driving back, with an assurance that I would come to know the truth, as I stayed focused on what I am doing. I just had to reach for the Spiritual Essence that I never knew before. I managed to stay calm as I drove. The tears flooded my lap yet cleansed my heart of all the resentment and fear I had been feeling all of my life. I began speaking out to myself as I drove; "I have a business to tend to and I can't allow myself to drop off into the deep, because of a dark past. I realize now for the first time in my life that I'm going to have to develop a calm and peaceful mind before I can have any closure."

I heard my mind speaking what is true as I drove back to my house, and I was finally convinced, I was only hurting myself. Ninety nine percent of the folks I thought hurt me had forgotten about it and the other ten percent knew nothing about it. I have to do something about making my own happiness."

"Uh, uhul, An Ole Luv Turns Up."

When I stopped by my Miami gallery to return calls and look over a stack of papers, and sign a few checks, I opened an e-mail from a past but just then my girlfriend popped in "Hey Jill, come on in." "Hey Sondra, did you just get back from your Moms?" "Yeah, have a seat. I was just checking my mail". "Is it anything interesting?" "Quiet interesting, Jill." Girl friend knew good and well who was lighting me up this way. I thought out loud, "An invitation to an Alaskan cruise with JOSH! Oh my God, I don't believe this!!!" Jill closed my office door. "Sondra, what are you going to do?" "I don't know right now. Girl, he was the best lover I ever knew and he almost became my husband." I was feeling hot and cold, and my thoughts were coming and going at the same time. I dare to consider. I'm thinking, I just learned I lost a twin sister at birth, and already, I am considering a cruise. My, this is a lot at one time. I gazed into my eyes in the mirror of my office powder room. My girl friend walked in behind me. "I'm just fine. Trust me." I sat down to relax for a moment. Just then, my secretary came in over the speaker phone and announced that I had a call holding on line one. She said, "You may want to take this call." That was our code for when one of those "male chemist calls" came in.

"Yes, this is Sondra." A familiar deep rich chocolate voice spoke "Sondra, Hi, this is Josh Simon, the one you left at the altar, remember? I hope you read my e-mail?" Hmmm, I had to clear my own voice and I almost was tempted to lie. "Oh Hi there, yes, Josh that was a very nice gesture, it's so good to hear from you. What's going on in your world? Are you getting married or am I too late for the wedding? "Funny. No, Sondra", "Hold on a moment Josh." My friend waved and left me in a private moment with the phone call. "I'm back." "No babe, I am not married and not getting married, unless you've reconsidered after all these years." Good thing I don't have the video telephone where he can see my face right now. "So tell me what's on your mind Josh?" I asked but having my own idea in mind. "You are on my mind Sondra." All right then!, Sondra's gleeful spirit blushed. "Josh, uhmm, I'm glad you thought about me. Let me get back to you about the cruise." "Come on lady, I'm not getting back to you for another round of your fun and games. I'm not going to take no for an answer, the cruise sails next month on the 15th and I want to fly you here to meet me, that way we can travel together baby." "It sounds wonderful Josh. I should be returning back from Egypt on the 13th, maybe I can just fly into ... Joel, where are you anyway?" "I'm in California love, I bought a condo just outside of a town called Kerrington Heights," Sondra's mind began to spin, thinking, if I hear one more thing about Kerrington today, I will just burst! "I'm living here now. I've made a complete career change and just signed a contract with a multi-billion dollar Corporation to design a mall in a near by town. I'll tell you all about it when I see you. I really want to see you pretty lady." Oh, he really knows how to turn me on.

"Listen, I'll meet you at the airport on the 13th, just call me the day before you leave. I gave your secretary my itinerary and information on how to reach me anytime, just in case." "Just in case what Josh?" "I'll tell you that too, when I see you." "Josh you are assuming I don't have anything going on in my life right now, that I can just swim away with you and we haven't spoken in, who knows when." "I know when. Sondra lets just say I have been keeping up with you, and giving you your space as you wished, at the same time. Now it is time you have a break and I want to discuss some things with you." "Well, you do have a point, and there may be some things we need to discuss, so I can't resist the invitation. I'll call you in a week or so." "Come on, I got to wait a week or so before hearing your sweet voice? I'll call you tonight before you go to bed, just to wish you a good night, sweet girl. Is that all right?"

All along I was noticing my resistance to the distraction of his every word and every tone of his delicious voice and every vision of his beautiful chocolate velvet body, hell, how could it not be all right. "That will be all right Josh. Talk to you later." "Later? Sondra, that is not soon enough, I'll talk to you in a few hours. Hey, I …" "Ah, Josh, I have a meeting starting in two minutes," "Sondra, I'll talk with you soon." *Click.* The phone went dead with no meeting starting in two minutes, just an exciting wait for the phone call to return.

"The Search Is On."

Oh, I can't stop thinking about Josh's and my conversation last night. My, that man sure has a way with me. But! I am determined to stay focused no matter what.

Auntie Clara met me at the airport in New York and we spent a good four hours together, she informed me of something that I must check into before coming back home. I know I'll be able to finally clear this web from my consciousness and be at rest with it. It's just dumb to run around in life literally puffed up at Ma, Pa, (who ever he is), and anybody else. It is really me I'm ticked off with because I don't want to let go of something that happened not just yesterday but too many yesterdays to count. Even the yesterdays in my relationship with men, especially with Josh, whom I was about to marry and settle for a wonderful life with the man I truly love, but I just let my past get in my way. I promise myself that when this is behind me I will consider marrying him, that is, if he will have me again. I do love him. He never asked me for anything except love. Oh my. Auntie has been a great inspiration to me in that I just have to make myself happy and the rest will follow. It's what I'm allowing to slow me down, while everybody else is moving on. Mama sure is. She saw me off after dinner and off I went on over to Egypt.

Wow, the heat hit me in Egypt quite hard but the Grand Opening celebration made up for it. A great success, everything went very well. I must say I am extremely thrilled to have found that the painting of Ma was sold to Josh Simon. He must be planning on surprising me. Like he said, he kept up with me. I see he has found my gallery even before it was hardly opened for business and before I could even get there. What a man. What was Josh doing in Egypt anyway, surely not checking up on me. Well I have a surprise for him, he's got to hand that painting right back over to me. The painting of mom is not for sale, even though he paid $17,000 for the picture. Heck, I have to give him his money back too? That was a nice chunk.

I got to give it to Mohammed, he sure bargains until he gets what he really wants. I might be off with my mother right now but she's all I got and besides I captured her in a moment when she was in a great mood to sit still.

Wow, Mama and this issue has been in my mind ever sense I left New York and had that talk with my auntie. It's been only a week here in Egypt but I got to go. Got to leave and get something settled right away. I'll get Mohammed to make my reservation changes and get right on in to California to check out these references Auntie gave me. Then I will really surprise Josh and be right at his front door when I call him.

I woke up when the announcement came that we were now coming in for a landing. Getting my overhead luggage and getting off, I became a little nervous about checking out the two sources auntie told me would have some information for me. Oh the butterflies in the pit of my stomach. Well, I better make the first call. That will be, let's see, to Ms. Jamie Cochran, let me get a bite to eat and a strong glass of wine. Better yet, I think I'll have a tall stack of strawberry pecan pancakes, Jill's and my favorite. I can just smell them. Um, um, um. Okay. Now I'm going to make that call. One ring, two rings, "Yes, this is Jamie." It was her. "Oh, yes, Ms. Jamie Cochran?" "Yes," "I am Sondra More, Christine More's daughter. My Auntie Clara" … I heard her say, "You don't have to go any further child, I know your mother. How are you, can I help you?" "Yes, I hope you can, I am just outside of San Diego right now, and I would like to see you. She then said "Oh, my dear, I would be so happy to feast my eyes on Christine's child." "I'm far from being her child anymore Ms. Jamie." "How is she anyway?" "Mother is doing fine." "Just call me Aunt Jamie child. Where are you anyway?" "I'm at a nice hotel called Kerrington Heights Quarters." "Then just give me one hour and I will be right over." I told her I would meet her in the lobby and I would be wearing yellow and black.

"Sondra." I looked over to my left and there stood a little short plump dark brown skin lady with silvery hair slicked neatly under a cute little black shinny straw hat, dressed like she was going to church. "Aunt Jamie?" "Yes, that's me." "Thank you for coming." "Lord, child I couldn't get here fast enough, you look like your mom. How did you say she was doing?" "Come on, we'll go up to my room, it has a nice terrace view of a beautiful lake.

"This is my first time being here since I was born, and that brings me to the reason I called you Aunt Jamie, not to beat around the bush. I don't want you to feel uncomfortable by the fact that I have not called you before now. You see my mother has been evasive with me around the facts of my birth and I want to know why. My auntie has told me that she and you talk from time to time and that you are willing to sit and talk with me on things that my mother may not. Auntie Clara said that you will not be violating Mother's confidentiality because you and she were the best of friends. "She is right, and I will do anything to be there for your Mother." "I appreciate you Aunt Jamie. I believe it would do Mother a world of good if somebody else would reveal the truth to me besides her, especially you." "Well Sondra, I will do my best to help you find your way."

"Aunt Jamie, I want to know who my father is of course, and if he is still alive here in California. I have no plans to invade or disrupt his life. Because of course I am sure he, that is if he is still alive, has a life of his own. To know he is still alive and what he is doing, what he is like, or even if he passed away, these kinds of things will at least help me to know myself better. Can you feel what I am saying?" "Oh yes, baby, I can imagine your heart's desire is to put this all behind you and go on with your life." "That is exactly what I want. I know mother would have told me but she could never get past her crying spells to tell me anything. So I would always just leave her alone. I can't imagine what could be so horrible that she had to leave him as she said, but I do know that I am strong enough to know and perhaps be a comfort to my Mother."

After rattling on and on, I looked closer over to Aunt Jamie and she had a blank look on her face. I asked her if she was all right, she assured me she was and that she would like to have something to drink. I told her there is some juice, milk and bottled water. She said she would like to have something a little bit stronger. "Okay, I know there is a bottle of wine here." "Okay, that will do." she said. I politely poured her a drink and she turned it all the way up. I knew I was about to get something here now. I don't know why I was surprised. Did she need this for encouragement to tell me something or was this some habit of hers?

Any way I asked if there was anything else I could get her. She said no, so I sat back down and made myself comfortable hoping she would become more relaxed too.

Maybe I too had better be prepared for this. I then refreshed my glass of wine. She began to say ... "Your mother was a very sweet girl as I recall when we were just in our early teens. We made plans to go away from home in Florida to visit my folks out here and work for the summer after we finished high school. We both loved to be around each other and we had the best times laughing and planning our future. She met a fellow she was so crazy about, he called her red bone, and she would get so mad with him. She liked him a whole lot. We also liked to write letters to our friends back home and tell them what a good time we were having even if we weren't."

"Jamie, I know you mean well, but I think I know Mom very well and Aunt Clara told me how she was as a child, she even told me about how she always wanted to leave Florida as a teen to live somewhere else and work for herself. I know she never went to college but fortunately she has prospered very well with her florist business and gave me the finest of what ever I wanted and needed."

"Jamie, I want to know what you know about my father. That is the bottom line." "Sondra, I pray to God that I am doing the right thing by telling you what I know. What you have asked of me, your Mother has never told me not to tell you anything." "If you don't feel in your heart that this is the right thing to do Aunt Jamie, please don't go any further." "No child, it is not fair for you to suffer for what choices others make." She held her glass out for me to take.

"Well there was a man that she was seeing quite frequently and that man loved the ground your mother walked on. He adored her so much and because of her he became very independently wealthy through self employment with high hopes that one day he would make her very happy. That man is Bobby Willis, the well known barber in Skyblue County California. I don't know if they kept in touch or not. Now like I said his business is across town and he would be very happy to meet you." "Are you alright Jamie? Can I get you something else?"

She scurried to get up. "You know baby, I really have to go somewhere very early in the morning, but I sure am glad we had this chance to meet. I got to go now." She hugged me tightly, picked up her purse and hurried out the door. I just sat and stared for a while wondering my next move, I threw myself across the bed and drifted off into a nap. I awakened freshly and grabbed the business pages. Look like ole Jamie has just led me on a wild goose chase.

"Getting Close"

Thumbing through the yellow pages, I found it. "Okay, here it is, Bobby's Barber," I called the number. Before I knew anything, he was answering, "Bobby's Barber, this is Bobby, may I help you?" Uhmm, yes, my name is Sondra and I would like to get a hair cut. There was a pause … Well, I am new in town and I would like to come over to meet you. Mr. Bobby, my name is Sondra, I am Christine More's daughter, and I still could use a hair cut." I was nervous. I could hear him breathing into the phone and not saying a word. Then he spoke, "Christine More's daughter?" "Yes, I would like to come over to meet you. Is that possible? I just want a moment to meet you sir." "Well, I am booked up right now … I could tell he was a little hesitant, and a lot surprised, I just couldn't tell if his reaction was positive or negative. "Well, where are you?" "I am staying at the Kerrington Heights Quarters." "Oh, I see, at Kerrington's place. Why do you need to see me? Is your Mother all right?" "Yes, she is doing well, still living in Florida." "That's good, so what are you doing here?" "You could say I am on a mission, Mr. Bobby." "You're a missionary?" "Well, I am on a mission for myself I guess I should say. I spoke with Ms. Jamie Cochran and she told me that you knew my mother. I would like to meet you before I leave to return to Florida."

"Why don't you come on over and we will have some lunch next door at the diner. Do you know where I am?" "Yes, I'll be there in no time." "See you then." "Thank you Mr. Bobby." He hung up and I fell across my bed exhausted with intense anticipation.

This is the hardest work I have ever done. You couldn't pay me enough to be an investigator into anyone's private life.

Mother sure made some choices that didn't make it so easy for me. I must learn a valuable lesson from this that the choices I make in life must be considering the effects of others. What a reality.

Okay, this must be the place. That must be the diner, and that must be him standing in the window waving at me, how he could know except that everyone says I look just like mom did at this age. He met me at the door. "My goodness, Sondra, you are the spitting image of your mother." "Thank you, I take it that is a compliment." "Yes, it is meant to be. Come this way, I have a table right over here." "Thank you for seeing me." "I was not expecting a call from Christine's daughter today, so please forgive me for sounding a little mixed up." "No problem, I will get right to why I wanted to meet you. I have never taken the opportunity to get to know the people who played very significant roles in my mother's life. It helps me to get to know myself better. Ms. Jamie told me that you were someone very special in my Mother's life." He had a serious look on his face as he set the record straight. "Oh, she certainly was to me and she always will be." As he spoke, I looked into his eyes; he had the saddest eye, and I thought I saw myself in them. I thought, could this man be my father and he doesn't know it?

Would it be why she left? He must have been a married man. That gold band looks mighty old on his finger. "Oh hell, I am just going to ask him. "Could it be that you are my father?"

All of a sudden he snapped out of it and looked at me with a big smile on his face and said, "My dear beautiful woman, you are far too beautiful to be my child, I wish I could say that you are mine. The fact is I know that you are not." Just then I felt a deep sense of disappointment. I realized I was having a hard time here. What and where to next? I thought. Should I give up here? But he said something comforting.

"Your Mother dropped me for someone of a lighter expression, and you are standing right at the front door to knowing who he is. It is not my place to make that information known to you my dear, when the time is right you will know. Don't worry your pretty little head. I love you as my own, because I still love your Mother. By the way, you still want that hair cut?" He said with a silly grin, trying to break the ice. It was getting kind of chilly and I was feeling really silly too.

"Let's eat something. What would you like?" During the lunch he told me of the business and how he had grown from one chair to eight and then to three shops with televisions installed for his customers and he was impressed also of the nature of my work expression. It was good of him to acknowledge Mother for being instrumental in his encouragement to go self employed. I shivered at the thought of what Mother would do if she knew I was sitting here talking to Mr. Bobby. "Bobby, I would like to get to know my father if he is still alive." He ate his food slowly, was quiet and began to stare across my shoulder.

What is up with everybody staring into space when I speak of my father? What's up with that? I questioned myself. I did not want to be too pushy so I too became quite. Just then, he spoke of a butler who my Mother was very close to at the estate where she worked. He said I might want to meet him and that he would see him the next day when he comes for a hair cut and would call me at the hotel to come over to meet him. I agreed, that would be just fine. On my way back to the hotel, I thought about Josh, but I wouldn't call him until I get a more information. I do have a couple of weeks here before I'm supposed to be here any way. Tomorrow I'm going over to the barber shop early, just in case Bobby gets busy, it is the weekend. Just as I was getting out of the rental car, I saw who thought could be the butler walking in. It was. Bobby introduced us. It turned out that they had spoken the night before that I had arrived in town. I had an intuitive feeling that the man knew my father and even knew me. What.. an.. eerie … feeling.

Later that day, I found myself visiting the estate where Mr. Jacob the butler, said my Father still lived. Driving up in a fine Bentley Limo I believe, I viewed the most beautiful sculptured grounds I'd ever seen. It was too exciting to realize that I was coming very close to closing the door on my dark past and opening a new door to the truth and the light of my being here. Yet this will make my life much more worth living. I'm keeping hope alive too.

"Revelations"

"Ms. More?" "Oh, Mr. Jacob, please call me Sondra" "Alright, Sondra. We are about to enter the estate through the servants' entrance, and I will announce you, is that all right?" "Mr. Jacob, who are you going to introduce me to?" "Well, my dear, Bobby and I spent all night discussing you and your Mother and the fact that you are searching to know your father. Obviously your Mother has not revealed that information to you and Bobby and I have loved your mother so very much. I contacted you Mother last night and …" "Wait, you had no right to do that Sir." "Please Sondra, your Mother and I keep in touch and she has informed me that you may reach out for the truth and that she trusts my handling of this situation. Would you like to speak with her yourself?" "No, as a matter of fact, I too, will trust your handling this situation. Thank you very much." "As I said, Sondra, your Mother has been like a child of mine, since the day she came to work as a manager for the horticulture department of the Kerrington estate. Your Mother was born with green thumbs and highly recommended to the Kerringtons." We both laughed quietly. "The day you were born I was there, and I saw the tears in your Father's eyes, I know the love he has for you. I know how much he has longed for this day although he agreed not to interfere with your Mother's life ever!" I was listening very intensely as Mr. Jacob spoke with assurance of what he was talking about. But I was getting a little weak in my knees, and somewhat a little irritable and decided to take a seat in his lavish quarters of the huge mansion as he spoke. I had quickly developed a deep sense of respect for this man. I am also getting the picture that he is not my father but that he knew him very well.

"Sondra, what I am about to tell you is going to be quite revealing and maybe shocking to you, so young lady sit back and try to relax, this could be a new beginning for your life and it certainly is in Gods interest that I tell you this." Oh hell, just tell me please. I thought to myself.

I also knew now that Mr. Jacob was a stern God-fearing religious man and I wasn't at this moment. He was about to get told off if he prolonged this one more minute. "God will be with you as He has been all along. You have nothing to fear my dear." As Mr. Jacob went on, I was really getting ticked off, yet anticipating a peace of mind of at last having a burden lifted from my shoulders if and when he said anything revealing and shocking.

"I am eager for what ever you have to tell me Mr. Jacob but just do it." He then sat down in front of me, took my hand and held it upon his knee. "Sondra, Mr. Joel Kerrington owns the city of Kerrington. People call it a city within a city." Well that makes sense to me, but what does that have to do with the price of potatoes? "Mr. Jacobs, it is occurring to me that there has been a lot of tele-phoning behind my back about my being here in Kerrington." "Yes there has been, and with your interest at heart. Mr. Kerrington had to be informed as well that you were in town." "And to what avail was that announcement?" "That everything is right on time and in everyone's favor. It is time. As I was saying, I have informed him that you are in town." "So I am now at his estate, what next? Really, I am not sure right now that I want to be here. Maybe I should go." "Sondra, Mr. Joel and I took a long walk in the garden and had a long thorough talk early this morning and he has prepared himself to meet you and so he informed me that … using his very words … he has long awaited this moment and he longed for it to be this way, that is, at the time of your choosing." With this build up, I was beginning to think Jacob was going to tell me I was born of Immaculate Conception and that God is my Father. Well now my breath began to feel heated up as he went on babbling. "There is much for you as well as the whole family to work out. Just remember you do not walk alone." Wow, I felt as though God *was* speaking to me now.

"I Go To Meet My Father."

Jacob began to rise from sitting in his quarters, and said in a swift soft voice, "Let us go now to meet your Father." I wondered did he really mean "The Father" or my Father. We walked out of his lodgings through an open courtyard of beautiful purple tulips, my favorite, and into the house. I wondered did Joel plant them over night because he knew I was coming. The house was just gorgeous. The furnishing was just what I would have chosen. Ah! Wait! I can't believe this. "Mr. Jacob, I pointed, where did that painting come from?" "What painting, Sondra?" I quickly walked over to the wall and felt my signature. It was the original painting that was sold in Egypt of mother. "This is my painting, how did it get here!?" I felt somewhat angry, yet puzzled. I wanted to take it down. I felt violated because of the way I had left mother and not meaning for the picture to ever leave my possession. "Calm down Sondra, It was a gift and you will soon know all that you need to know shortly. Come with me." I tried to calmed myself and trust the moment to know what was to come. I walked his way. This had better be gooood. I murmured under my breath between gritting teeth.

Now we were reaching the end of a long wide corridor of a bright green floral plush carpet that led into a huge sun room. There stood a very handsome olive tone tall well built man. I then knew. It was he. The man I had longed for all of my life, really and finally. A peaceful rush came out to greet me all through my limbs and I fell numb to the floor. When I realized a few minutes had gone by, I was looking into his eyes from the corner of a couch. He was kneeling over to me and gazing into my face.

"Welcome home Sondra," and most oddly enough the action and words he spoke, I knew were the exact action and words being spoken to me by the Great Spirit of my own soul. It was like, "Now you and I can spend some time together as One." In that beautiful moment, it was not about him or me. It was about that Great Spirit within me. She was always with me.

He continued to stand hovering over me as though he thought if he moved I would fall off the couch or get up and run away. I don't remember getting up but we were both walking out to a near by pond. The sun seemed to beam only where we walked. I looked up at him and asked, "So you are my father?" "Yes my love."

He had tears in his eyes as he looked at me with a smile on his face. We embraced for what seemed eternal as I read the thoughts in my head silently. "Why, didn't you want to be with me and mom? Didn't you know I longed to grow up with you and feel the cradle of your arms, to smell you and to hear your voice? To walk with my hand in yours and to see you at my most endearing events, to learn your ways and to know I would see you at night? I missed that in my life."

I felt him weeping inside as though he read my thoughts. I too, began to sob with him. I later felt guilt of my thoughts when he began to answer them all in just a few brief sufficient words. Then I stepped back to look into his beautiful aging face and allowed him to speak to me more. All along I could feel at the same time and hear that Great Spirit answer, "You have never lacked any thing. Your Mama was always there with you and for you. What is all this I 'need' you; I 'miss' you about? Even your Uncle took care of you and your Auntie fed you encouragement, hoping you could see you didn't miss a thing. You only wanted what you saw and heard about your little friends and their daddies. Your mama used to tell you, We have given you everything; what do you think you need that you don't have?" Now you have met the man that was partner with your mom at the time of your conception. What now?" We both stood and stared as though he could hear everything that was being read in my head. I had nothing more to say, nor did he at that moment. There was great magic in that moment, a moment of a lifetime.

"The Secret Told"

He walked over to the garden chair and sat down with his face in his hands being silent. I then prayed in silent into myself for thanksgiving and the relief this moment was bringing. He then began to explain. "Sondra, the answer to your questions are not brief I know." My thought then was "Oh but I do know that anything you could say will be the chalice I must drink from as I feel the sincere welcome from your heart." "If you will allow me, you will know why you have not known me as the father you were deprived of. The truth of the moment, I did know why. He continued.

"First I have to tell you who else you have not known." I felt I knew the answer to that one, which It has been my wonderful Goddess Self that I have not known. All of a sudden there was no apology needed from anybody. No words, deeds, or actions were needed to boost the now moment. This enduring Self of us is the battery that keeps us going no matter what. I had lived a half of a lifetime externally. I came out of my amazement to hear him say. "Your mother has been suffering because of this, but you must never hold it against her." Heck, I thought she only suffered because she thought I was suffering as I kept this in her face and mind for that long. "Forty two years ago she had no choice in the matter as it has turned out and forty two years ago she and I chose to love one another and bring forth two beautiful healthy girls." he said. "Oh, my, God." I said louder than I realized. "Don't tell me you were in on this secret of another sister."

"Now she will have the joy of her life to be reunited with her other daughter, your twin sister, Sylvia." Wait a minute!, I thought, I missed something, I must have been absent in my thinking for a longer moment than I thought.

"Did I hear you to say something about reunited with the other daughter? my sister? Is she ... is she not dead? I mean, did she not die at birth?"

"Jacob, will you have Sylvia to come please." "Yes, I will." "While he is gone for Sylvia, I will tell you this and tell you both later. There has been a lie that the Kerrington family has lived with since you were born." I feel ill now. Lies, what else is new? Is there any truth in all of this? "The source of that lie is dead." God, I am glad that I wasn't around. He went on and on. "Now that you have re-entered Kerrington, Sondra, the lie dies as well." What on earth is he talking about? As soon as this revelation is clear, I am out of here. I am taking my portrait of mama with me too. "Yes, and who, what, where, and why is my mother's portrait in this house? I sent it to Egypt. Who bought it and brought it here? I want the truth about that too."

He looked up towards the door behind me and said "Sylvia …, it is time for you to meet your twin sister, Sondra." I don't know who fainted first, me or her. No, really, we both stood in shock and flopped down on the couch at the same time. We were twins all right. I was Seeing Double.

The next thing I knew, we were both sitting on the chair by the pond holding on to the wrought iron chair for dear life. Jacob was sitting between us. I noticed him wiping his bald head and when I looked past him to Sylvia … I knew I was SEEING DOUBLE. I looked up at Joel as he had pulled a chair over to the couch to be near us all for support. He was lost for words and began speaking but I didn't have all of my senses back especially my hearing. This was a lot too much for me in one day. I really mean in one life time. Worst was, these people were of another culture, I am not sure what.

I know I asked for this, I came to know what was meant by the phrase "you better be careful what you ask for." If I may add "and be prepared for the way it will come." I realized it was a shocker for all the others as well. I had millions of questions but at the moment I just wanted to be still and hold on to the answers I had just gotten. I was ready to have it all be over and NOW get on with life. I realized that I now just had to find a way to say, "Okay now, we can all get back to what we were doing before I walked in. Or better, before I became 10. I felt like saying "I want my Mama." Man when you are ready, I mean really ready, the truth will kick your ass and set you free at the same time. With the quickness that you think you have something better to do.

For really real, I just wanted my Mama to tell her, "Mama, we had it made, I just wish I could have been content with the way it was. Let us just get on with our lives and walk the yellow brick road together." I feel this woman Sylvia is happy in her other world with her, our Father. As for Mama, I know she would just look at me, like I just found my right mind, give me a hug and go right back to her garden.

I felt I had opened a door to a bunch of tigers that all wanted to attack me but ran past me to play with the lions.

We were all quite for a few minutes until I heard Sylvia say, "Uncle Joel, what are you saying to me?" I thought I was listening to myself speak. He said to her, "Sylvia, give me a minute." "No!" She shot to her feet and stood up over him. "I want an explanation, Now!, What is going on here?" Jacob, the butler, stood up beside her and asked her to sit down and listen to Joel, that he is doing the best he could under the circumstances. "Just listen." Sylvia focused her statement to me of what she really wanted to know … "Who are you, (looking me dead in my face) to come into our home and create this madness of confusion?" She sat down and I listened as best I could without thinking of Mother. Wait, woe, did I just hear her say, Joel? She's been thinking all this time "Daddy" was who? Man, this family was sitting on a pack of lies in all their wealth. "Well my Mama certainly is not responsible for any of this neither am I. I just want an explanation myself and I will be history to you all. I did not come here to visit or to stay." Jacob again ushered me back into my seat. I sat on the cushioned long chair, big enough for four people to sit in a curved fashion. Joel sat in front of the three of us. "Sylvia, the family has been living a lie since you and your sister were born." I didn't have to wonder why any more. "You were taught to believe a lie. Now the truth will be told. Although I never lied to you, I never told you the truth either." Now he's gonna tell somebody the truth. "Sondra and Sylvia, I have suffered for that, I just hope you can accept what is true after your 42 years have gone by and I pray you can forgive me and everybody involved." I was not only ready to forgive. I was one second from forgetting. It is forgotten. Just give me my painting and I'm gone.

I wished they could read my mind right about now. We both were sitting lifeless while Jacob sat between us as though he was a hired referee or maybe he was our great old granddaddy and I wouldn't be surprised if that was the next surprise.

"The Confession"

"Sondra, Sylvia", Oh here it comes … "your Mother was my first love and will always be" ummm … well that sounds original. "Who is my Mother?" asked Sylvia. That was an intelligent question. I feel better conversing with my self. I wondered how he was going to answer that. "Sylvia, you will meet her soon." Not if I can help it, I thought. I've got to find a way to cut this off. "She is Catherine More." Sylvia just sat there in awe staring at a Kleenex. "This is why I have never taken a wife since you two were born." Oh, he and Mother must have been planning on getting together in the after life. "At that time we were not allowed to get married." Man this awakening moment is what must be the "twinkling of the eye", because I sure am glad everything happened just the way it did. Mama and I had a good life together, after all. He continued. "I was the youngest son of the two boys. Your Mother was hired as a staff member at the time of revamping the estate. My Mother died when I was 15 of food poison and Father married his secretary a few years later. My Step Mother loved your Mother until she became pregnant. I thought to myself, who became pregnant, my Mother or your Step Mother? He answered my thought. "Your Mother became pregnant of course.

My Step Mother went into a rage for days and weeks until she convinced Father, since they would not allow us to marry, to take care of Catherine, your Mother for nine months as mother faked that she adopted one of you from an agency and they sent your Mother away with you. She left reluctantly and I promised her we would be reunited later. In those times there was not much she could do. My Step Mother passed away when you girls were twenty and your Mother decided to have nothing to do with me. She didn't know how to explain this to the two of you." I was exhausted from the story and thinking, so that is why she said she lost the other twin at birth.

"Dad died two years later than my step mother. Catherine still would not see or speak to me. I was afraid of loosing all I would have had in the future to take care of you girls and your Mother, had I left with your Mother when she became pregnant. I have always loved Catherine and always will." So the step woman couldn't have anyone know he had knocked up a house servant and he wanted to marry her too. Joel said, "Our Step Mother ruled this house." I see. "Unfortunately, my Grandfather gave his mind over to her dominance." I was thinking, Sondra, if Bobby the barber had been your father, you would not be sitting here in this stew right here, right now. My Father could have been sweet little old black Bobby the Barber. Whew! Joel went on with face in his hands. She would forbid Mother to leave the house in her showing months, for fear of a scandal and because she loved Joel so much. "When you were born right here in this house, she gave Catherine a bank account to leave and take you with her." Well thank you. Thank you very much the step Grandmother. I had a good life after all. I am sorry for you Sylvia and that we didn't get to know each other. But Oh Well. That is life. Mama, you won't have to hold this any longer. I have made some choices. I started to get up when he continued crying, "She also paid to have your birth certificate state you were born in Florida." He looked at me in his hour of confession, "Sylvia was raised as her child and as my very young baby sister." Man, what a sick twisted saga. Well, I came, I've conquered, and I must go. I Know I would have been further up this road, if I had just kept on a walking up the Goddess's Highway. Do you mind, I'd like to be left alone for a moment." Joel answered, "Sure." He seemed surprised how I was taking all this. He just didn't know that Mama prepared me for this in the way she raised me. Now I can see that.

They all looked at me as Jacob asked if I was all right. I answered. "I'm fine. Just want to call my mother." Jacob walked out and I followed. As we walked further away from Joel and Sylvia, I could hear them talking back and forth with each other. "Jacob, have I made a mistake in coming here?" "Nothing is ever

"Mis" taken in life Sondra. We just take the consequences for that come to put us back on track."

Another interrupting thought was about how crooked the old lady was. I heard Joel tell Sylvia, "I was forbidden to try to contact your Mother or I would be cut off from the family and I knew I would have no means to support your Mother or the two of you. There was no way around it considering the racial tension in that time. Your Mother was taken care of by my Brother who is five years older and ran the major part of the business. As their voices faded I thought, Good for us, your big brother, my Uncle was in my corner.

"Jacob, I would like to call my Mother right away." Jacob has been by my side every step of the way. I looked back and saw my Father was sitting back as though he had emptied a load of bricks from his chest and needed someone on his side to haul them away. Sylvia looked nauseated and excused herself.

As she left the room I felt her tremendously. That was the other side of me leaving. That was okay. We were not Siamese Twins. I had to relax myself and rest the spinning wheels in my head. I could all of a sudden feel a great dust storm settling for all of us.

My Father's brother walked by the door where Jacob left me, he came over to me and handed me a glass of fresh orange juice and planted a kiss on my forehead. I knew who he was. I felt he knew me as well. He was cool with me, especially sending us all that money through the years.

During the silent moment, I had one question in particular for him. Softly I asked. "May I ask how that painting of my Mother got on your wall out there?" "Yes," my Uncle spoke up and said, "A client of mine just returned a week ago from Egypt and had that picture sitting in his office. I asked where he got it and who is the artist? He told me a young lady that he loved very much painted it. I recognized Catherine's beautiful face, and I told him that Catherine once was a staff member and was responsible for the designs of the gardens here at Kerrington. Before he told me your name and I gave him a blank check for it and told him I knew of the artist and had to have it. He gave me the check back and told me it was a gift. I took it and now it is a gift back to you." I forced a smile. "Does Josh know any of this?" "No he absolutely does not. I did though invite him on a cruise that now you are very much a part of." I thought, I sure am, with an invitation that came long before all of this did, it must have been a preordained future event.

I took a deep breath as I felt the comfort of Jacobs' hand placed on mine. I don't know when he wondered back in and sat beside me. "How am I going to tell my Mother any of this?" I was beginning to worry. I heard the next words coming from Joel again, as he too had come over to James's area of the mansion. I didn't see Sylvia though. "Sondra, I have spoken to Catherine already." My next thoughts were how and when? I've been with you all day. It was amazing. He continued …, "Jacob and I spoke with her early this morning before he came for you. Jacob has been in touch with your Aunt and she informed him that you may be coming this way. She felt that you and your Sister must know the truth and that this would free the family at last." Wow, I asked … "What is she saying about all of this?" "She is elated and somewhat relieved. She wants to meet Sylvia, only if she wants to know her. Your Mother is a very strong woman. I assured her everything will be perfect. The staff has already prepared your quarters and we will all come together again." He is so right about the strength of my Mother. Too bad Sylvia couldn't have been around Mama in her growing up years.

I couldn't help but be concerned about Sylvia. She does not accept what has been revealed. I was prepared for it all of my life, because I knew within my heart that there was another part of me living on this earth expressing a part of myself. Finding out who you thought was your Step Brother is really your real Father, and that whom you thought was your real Mother was really your Step Mother. That is not quite revitalizing. I stood for a few moments and stared out of the window into a huge swimming pool and Joel stood up and held me very close in his arms. He reached out to Sylvia and she rejected him. Joel looked over at Jacob and I could read that Sylvia was going to need help and very soon. Joel walked out to find Sylvia. My void was now beginning to be filled. I was really ready to fly south for the warmth of my Mother's arms.

Jacob stood up and asked if I would like to have some time along. I nodded and walked away. He told me that Mother would be arriving the next morning. I decided to just stay in the room and have some fruit, freshen up and lie down as he suggested. At that moment, I felt a rush of comforting joy surge through my being, as though I had just been placed on top of the world.

This is something I had begged for all of my life. O my, this is some kind of happiness I am feeling this day. I found out who is my Father and that there is another expression of myself who is beautiful and is going to find healing as I have. I will be there for her when she is ready.

I looked out through the window that faced the east where we drove up the driveway coming in. The sun rose on my back early this morning as I came in to the place where I was born and left with a very saddened mother, torn apart from the sibling that shared the same womb, to leave her to face a lie that would test her life as well as mine, whether to pass or fail when the truth would finally come. In that time of forty plus years that seemed like such a long time, in Divine time it is only a blink of an eye. Now healing comes, the experience then seems like it was just yesterday. Now the same sun rises again for me, knowing that I will know that our job will be to use the wisdom of this experience to enhance the rest of our life and be a warm rising sun to others in those cold stabbing moments of time to be melted by a fiery furnace of Truth.

Here I will lie down again in that place awaiting my Mother this time, not to tare me away from myself but face another rising sun of togetherness in divine truth and celebration of my Divine Self. I was born a traveler. I've since traveled east, west and back east again. Now I am in the west, soon to go back south. Home really is where the heart is.

The knock at the door scared the heck out of me that moment. I quickly got up and wrapped the silk robe around me with the letter "K" embroidered on it next to my heart, in gold thread. "Ms. Sondra, the driver is arriving with your mother." "Oh thank you." Wow I am in joy in this morning. Why didn't someone wake me earlier? I wondered. After praying in the most beautiful sunrise, I began to look for what to wear. I got my bath and was ready to greet Mama in no time. Mama and I made up like we always do and this time it was as though we were together for the first time in 42 years. She also had her day with Sylvia and I think they are going to be just fine. On the third day as I prepared for another new day, I spoke to the server "Today I must call on Josh! After all, it's getting close to the date to leave for the cruise. I'll shock Josh with my connection to the Kerringtons and I can't wait to see the look on his face when he finds out how small our world really is." She just smiled at my joy. I'm sure there is talk among the staff about all that's been going on here.

"The Big Surprise"

"Josh, hi, its Sondra, I am right here in Kerrington. I thought I would surprise you and come on in. Would you like to meet for brunch at 12:30?" "Well, let's see, how about the pancake house in town?" "Good, then I'll see you there at 12:30."

Seeing Josh will make things really okay. There he is, what a wholesome looking man. He doesn't see me yet. Oh my goodness. His hair has grayed gorgeously, with a beautiful mature gray beard on that rich carob brown skin. Muscles fully developed in all the right places. He is tall enough for my eyes to look up to. My. My. My. Now I know, if there *was* a man named Adam, he must have looked like my Josh. I have been looking for him for quite sometime especially after realizing I have to be what I am looking for. Sondra EVE is my name. I mean … Let me quit. I'm being silly now. He really looks good being a distinguished older man.

Oh he has spotted me. I've got to compose myself. We both extended our arms and embraced very warmly. Yes indeed. Josh led me to our table. He was very complementary and hummmm, I don't know what his intentions are but I do know mine. I just want to be at peace, starting with a clear mind.

We had a nice day. I got some shopping in for myself, Mom, my Father, Uncle, Sister and Jacob. I also got a "lil sompin" for Aunt Jamie, Bobby and Auntie Clara. I found Mama a gold bracelet with our favorite saying, "Nothing is ever lost." Josh will get his gift later, maybe. Ha ha. We parted with a kiss and I returned back to the mansion. Josh still doesn't know what he is in for in a few days. My Father was there to greet me when the Limo pulled up into the driveway. He gave me a very warm hug and said that Sylvia was looking for me and that she wanted to spend some time with me. From what I gathered about her, I am the more out going one and more expressive in thoughts and action. She seems more of a recluse and somewhat secretive. There are two sides to everything, an up side and a down side. When we are conscious we can stay on the up side. Only time and experiences will unravel and reveal what is real. I am sure Sylvia knows more than she lets on to.

"Sondra, now that we have come together as a family, what are your plans?" I had to pause for a long moment to search myself for the answer to her question and I was not sure that I wanted to give her an answer right then. "Sylvia, I really can't answer that right now. But I am sure you will love my answer. I don't plan to crowd your space. Is that your worry?"

"No, not at all, I just want to..uh.." "I know, you want to know if I will be in the way of you and Josh." A long pause as she looked in another direction. "I can't hide my feelings for him from you, can I?" "You don't have too." She interrupted the silence with a laugh I noticed I use when I do wish to hide something but can't. "Sylvia, first, I would like to give you something I picked up today for you? It is just something I feel will express my love for you as my Sister. I also got the same for Mother." "I got her a diamond bracelet watch, with our two emerald birth stones."

She looked at me for a long moment and took the bracelet, still staring at me. I said, "It's okay isn't it?" "You didn't have to Sondra, I really just desire to go on living the way I was before. With all that has come out and even though ..." "Even though what?" "Even though you seem to be the Sister I always wished I had, I have developed a feeling for Josh only after speaking to him by phone and seeing him from a distant when he was here at a meeting with Joel. I will find a way to be with him." "Without my being in the picture, I'm sure." "Well Sondra, after all I never knew you existed." "But now you do. Listen Sylvia, I was supposed to have married Josh some years ago before you knew him and I have realized the loneliness I created in not doing so. He has opened that possibility again to me recently and I don't know if you could ever be that important to him. I'm getting that some part of you may only remind him of me as he does not know our connection. I think we should let him make that decision him self." "I agree Sondra. He will have to make that decision and he will have the opportunity while on the cruise." "Yes, he will, Sylvia." "Sondra, will you be leaving after the cruise?" "It all depends."

"You know, we do have some similarities, I dabble in the arts myself. I love reading and writing as well." "Yeah, and I see we also have the same taste in men." "Ah, yeah, we do, don't we?" "Yes, we do. We have the same taste in the same man." It will be interesting what Josh's appetite will be for this weekend. Well, I better grab my things and get ready to go. "Don't worry Sylvia I know everything will work out just fine." "So do I."

"Mother is certainly not a difficult person to get along with, in spite of her deep wounds and disappointments. She just needs to know that she is loved and forgiven for the choices she has made in life as she learns to love and forgive her self."

Now I know this cruise is going to be an interesting one with twin sisters loving on the same man, who has no idea what is the plan, nor what cards are in his hand. I'm really not worried. She is beautiful, and almost as classy as I am but I am prepared for what ever happens.

The big day came when we were gathered at my Father's private landing pad on top of the big mansion, to fly out for the big 7 day cruise. It seemed the big contest was on. Sylvia was more beautiful than I could imagine. Her cabin was lined with the ambiance of romance. I had forgotten what that was. Well I had better remember. I do intend to marry this man. I excused myself from her cabin and rushed to mine to lay out what I was going to wear on our first evening and the next evenings to follow. Well … Mr. Josh made his appearance, God what a chunk of a Man-ifestation he is. I walked out to greet him for the first time in three days, but it had been 8 years prior to that. I was beginning to feel heated up. "Hi Josh" "Sondra, you … look … ravishing." He held me close and pressed a warm kiss on my pouting lips. "Josh, meet Sylvia." "I believe we have met." Josh in shock, stood and stared. We both allowed him to relish the moment until he came back with "Who are you!? You two know each other?" Josh was pointing to our faces. "You look like twins almost."

"Well Josh, as a matter of fact we do know each other. And under very strange circumstances we *are* twins." "Woe. Woe. Woe. Wait a minute. What do you mean Sondra?" "Josh, I am Sylvia Kerrington. Joel hired you to build for him." "Yes that's right." Yes, she is a beautiful plus size woman, I will say she looks just like me except she is about 3 shades lighter beyond my complexion and her hair is a medium straighter dark curly bronze to compliment her olive complexion and hazel eyes. My eyes are the shade of my dark brown hair and much curlier. My rear seems to be a little fuller.

"Josh, are you okay baby, do you need to sit down? You look like you just met a ghost face to face." He then took me by my hand and pulled me over to the railing and asked me between his teeth. "What is going on here Sondra? I spoke very loudly and out of control, "Joel, Sylvia is my twin sister." My frustration was about to spill over. He turned a bright shade of purple. "What!" he said, "Yeah, I got to sit down," He went to take a seat on the deck as Sylvia and I followed looking at one another with astonishment, though we both were in awe as to how he was taking this. I know what was going on in my head but unfortunately not hers. After all, we are not identical twins. Thank God.

Josh stared at us both back and forth as though he was expecting one of us to disappear. Sylvia asked, "How long have you two known each other?" Joel waited for me to speak, so I did. "We were once lovers." He took a deep swallow and stated … "I'd like a drink, what about you guys?" Sylvia said she didn't drink. I asked the bar tender to give him a shot of scotch and me a glass of brandy. Then there was silence and I heard others talking. Sylvia asked "How long ago was that?" and looked at Josh for the answer. "Oh, about 10 years, wasn't it Sondra?" "Something like that Josh." "What about you guys?" Josh asked of Sylvia and me. "We've been together a little less than a week now" I answered. "Okay, are you going to tell me what's happening or what?" "I will tell you darling. Sylvia, Joel, John and I just met again. We last saw one another exactly 42 years ago when mother was living in Kerrington before we were born. There was a separation and now we are here together again. We're now one big happy family, how about that?" Joel was a little bit at ease now. "Yeah, how about that?"

We then all started to speak again at the same time, when just in time, someone interrupted us pointing for us to look to our left at the new mall that was being constructed, for which Josh had drawn the blue prints. The air became thin and at ease as we went in for dinner, dancing and finally off to our separate rooms. I leaned over, pecked him on his cheek and said my good night to him and Sylvia. As I walked away, they chatted and I disappeared. They thought. From around the corner of the deck I saw her move closer to him and began chatting away in his face, getting closer and closer then pull him towards her room. Oh, is that the way she plays? Silvia's room was across the hall from mine and I watched him enter her cabin from my peep hole. 10 minutes became 1 hour. My eye was about to fall out. He left her cabin without his coat and without his tie. Obviously he didn't know where my room was. I wasn't worried though. I knew he had to make a choice.

By the forth night he asked if I would join him in a game of scrabble on deck. That was our game. I accepted the invitation. He let me win, I know to cut the game short then he said he had to make a phone call. "Josh, what is your hurry?" "Well our time is short here and I need to clear some things and make some plans for next week." I tried to give him a kiss but he rushed off. I spoke out. "You know Josh you can have her here and me when you are in Florida. I know the choice is hard to make." He looked back in surprised at my offer. "I will have who I choose and that's it." I knew when I gave him the freedom to choose, he could make up his mind then. "You and your sister are very beautiful and youthful, I have made my choice and I can't live without it. I have chosen one who is totally a charm to my heart and I have watched her from afar. I don't want to go on without her any longer." I hope you both can deal with my decision." "We both agreed we would Josh." I thought I heard a twist in his little speech but I understand he is a little confused right now. I tried for a kiss again but it didn't work. "Why don't I tell you both together?" "Fine, Josh you don't sound like yourself." "I know I feel like someone new." "Wow" "That's what I've been saying all week. I will announce my choice at breakfast." "Okay then. Sounds like a done deal, Josh, if that's the way you want it." "That's the way I want it Sondra, with no hard feelings." "Fine, a kiss good night, Josh?" I stepped away then I stepped back close to Josh and surprisingly enough, he shocked me and stepped away with that Denzel walk of his and without a kiss. He's up to something.

The final morning I met mom coming from the room of Sylvia and I complimented her on how good she smelled and looked and how happy she seemed. She gave me a tight hug and said, "You're going to be much happier when you know why I smell, look and feel so good." Oh … I thought she and dad had something up their sleeves. Mom knew I was happy to be my own independent self and I know she wished I would consider dating again. She never knew I was in love with Josh and I never needed to tell her especially since she had not had anybody in years, so she said. I just needed her to focus on herself.

We arrived for breakfast where everybody was waiting. Wow, I slept late because after all this excitement, I felt exhausted. After today, we all will return to our own personal lives … but this time as new ones. I know Josh and I are going to be so happy this time. Sylvia will be all right, after all they have only known each another for a few weeks. Things look so different now that I have settled my life long quest. The Gallery up and running in Egypt and all. Josh walked towards me as I reached out to him and he took mothers hand and nicely led her to her chair as she glowed all over her self. He is such a gentleman. Sylvia took a seat beside him and I took the one across from him. Joel seated the woman he invited, I guessed another business partner and John was with his notebook, his cell phone, checking his agenda for the rest of the month. Probably for the next five years. Joel stood up and we all looked at him as he began to give the Thanksgiving prayer in June. I mean he was truly thankful … finally we began to have breakfast. After breakfast, what seemed to take just as long as the prayer to finish, Josh stood up. We all looked up in surprise, wondering if he to was going to pray, make a toast or what? But, he was about to make an announcement of some sort. Oh gosh, my Josh. Was this it? Sylvia and I have been waiting for this. We both tried to smile but the elasticity in our faces just broke. Well, whatever, I am prepared for this, after all I've been through, I can take anything.

"Excuse me ladies and gentlemen," he tapped his spoon against his water glass, "I have a very important announcement to make. I could not think of a more appropriate time than now to express my gratitude for being alive and being included into this family, not just as an associate partner but also as a friend of this great family. Thank you John, Joel." He nodded at them both. "In meeting someone for the first time in person, after having a picture printed in my heart and mind of such a refined and exciting woman. I choose to not let any more time get away from this precious moment. Life finally has given me a choice of a lifetime and I must make it now. I feel that she knows my deepest feelings for her, in sending my greatest telepathy to show her as she has mutually shown her feelings for me over these few days, I took the opportunity of this cruise to become reacquainted with her and I'm asking her to fulfill the rest of mine and her days together. This most beautiful woman in my midst is … The beloved … Catherine More." No he didn't! He said … wait a minute, I, I couldn't hear him clearly, somebody, what is happening here? it seems like a frozen moment of still silence, everybody with locked faces of frozen smiles. "What? What did he just say?" I looked around to see if any one heard what I thought he just said. I softly asked Sylvia, "Did he, did he just call out my Mother's name?" She looked like she didn't hear me at all. I looked from person to person and quickly to my Mother, then what appeared in slow motion was him taking her hand, pull her up from the table and draw her close to him and kiss her. Not on her cheek but on her mouth. She was who I thought he said, "My MOTHER!" I shouted before I passed out. It seemed like a week in a coma when I returned to my senses to learn that I went out as I was trying to hold on to hear Josh finish saying

"Catherine More's beautiful daughter Sondra but I heard right. Josh chose my Mother Catherine More."

The great moral of this story's sweet ending is this:

Though in the many facets of life we face, approaching many cross roads, we have to choose which road to take next. When not being open to our intuition to choose the way best for our journey, it turns out that the way chosen is also the right way. That is what I call The Great Mother in me. Mother knows best. Remember the pre-sent moment? Always there until we become awakened to know, what we see as doubles or this and that, or me and God, turns out to be only one. The True Self, the Gift we send ourselves unknowingly for thinking the unawareness comes from the external Self. We are constantly speaking that has been sent by word or thought and then we walk into the moment.

Introduction to the story of
THE GARDEN OF EVE

As a result of this second story, I made an extraordinary metamorphosis of an illusionary delusion and allowed myself to heal by returning to the love I already had.

We create life experiences only to focus our lens on ourselves and where we are really headed in life. Our life experience is the stuff on our lens that we just need to get real and wipe it off to see what is really going on. Stay in the moment.

I will give you a realized parable of an experience that gave me the opportunity to heal a drained soul and return to Pure Love once again.

On my first journey to "Africa," my quest broke me all the way down and I do mean I had to "Break Down" just to build myself up again in the proper way. My ego showed up as a desperate victim and not the empowered woman that I truly am. Refusing to see clearly because of anger, I began to sacrifice the reality of Love by focusing of the negative energy of a failing relationship.

Our hearts desire can come just to prove that yes, like does attract after its kind. We find ourselves with a desire for the perfect union, with perfect family and not fully knowing what that is like and not taking the moment to design it for ourselves.

Our dreams and desires can bring us nightmares that cause us to struggle to wake up. We have opportunities to examine our Self with the power of choices in every event of our life that would make us the Cinderella of our own ball.

Examine closely what choices you make and the consequences you are drawing to you to draw you closer to your Greatness. Hopefully the outcome will be that you never need that experience again.

Our personal lives are filled with "stories," we just have to remember that we are not our stories, we have them to share with others allowing them to know the same, to grow and not allow ourselves become possessed by our stories. It is my knowledge that all stories we have read of biblical events, no matter what religion, when we hear them as mere allegories we don't get caught up sitting at the red light thinking of what happened to the person and missing the green light, we can get the message and move on up the road to divine empowerment. The greatest stories ever told, reveals the greatest Truths life holds. This is the essence of the purpose of my sharing with you, for your own soul integration of oneness with The Creator.

The journey of what seemed to be way over a Kazillion steps began shortly after leaving the shores of "home." Eve was threatened a "bash over her head" as her man had promised her in the land of Africa. Thanks to him the promise was all that was needed to put the Goddess on her path to journey of awakening. This was to be her wake up call ... Eve had rather have been a standing tall Witch, ready to be burned alive at the stake than to continue as a "wife" to this verbally abusive, bully for a mate. She realized later that with her initial resistance to enter into this relationship, was her soul screaming that there was nothing to heal only truth to be revealed. Therefore, she created the experience to prove that.

When we choose not to remember our own power we surrender to the suppression as submissive little zombies. Let the so called sick relationships turn into healthful ones with choice, until you have enough sense (will power and Self esteem) to Love your Self.

Have a "Sankofa Experience" for yourself, review your past experiences for a moment or just look at the "now moment" the "present" or (pre-sent) for an awakened moment of what you are creating for your own self awareness. In a Sankofa Moment is the greatest Gift you could ever give to yourSelf. What I mean by "pre-sent" is that The Great Cosmic Mother God has already sent us all the presents for our final destination along the road to Her. All we have to do is to open them and "See" with our Spiritual Eye, the Gift. In the event we don't see, but we see with the "ego" eyes, we may have to remain on the square until it is our turn to go further. Frustration blurs the vision. Strive to remain peaceful and the solution of knowing what to do next will open that Eye to See the way.

Many of our closely attached acquaintances are effected by the karma we experience from the seeds we have sown (choices we have made) prior to its reward.

The journey to the continent with the new found Love mirrored that the lack of love for ones Self shows up in a partner who doesn't love their Self, therefore each mirrors the other. He was destroying himself through an addiction and so was Eve for the addiction to external love. When we reach into the mirror to brush our teeth, what happens? The ones in our mouth remain dirty.

This story is not about Adam but about Eve and what led her to heal her blindness to see what power lies within herSelf. Eve was not seeking to remove any mote from his eye when she felt she had a lumber yard in her own that kept her from seeing what was revealing itself now. We fool and handicap our knowledge of "Self" when we look to others for security and survival, denying the flaws of our dirty lenses. When we do clean our consciousness of the dirty froth that won't allow us to show pure unconditional Love or show forgiveness to those we struck out in anger with ourselves, we become ourSelf and move up and onward in Life. I don't want to miss the opportunity for that someone showing up in my life with a pure and clean heart.

As women who have descended so far from the once Powerful Matriarchal System we once knew, our rise is the secret of the cosmos. We are moving out of the land of illusions and we are reaching out to take the blind folds off of others.

Eve is striving to resurrect herself to her calling again, since the feminine energy has been down played to just being birth canals only as though that is not powerful enough within it's self. Eve tried to wash the words quoted by this Adam from her head that his secret lover was only to him a "come dump." Is that the general view of other men today? "Mother, help Adam or take him away." Women have had to be their own "Help Mates" as far as carrying the load of a balanced relationship. Having the capability to do it all anyway, being complete within herself. The self that we think can't make it alone, is our own denial of our own illusionary illness and the denial of our own innate power. Eve can make it alone but why should she?

The need of codependents is serious denial and an excuse to blame something or someone external to ourselves as though we are not equipped with what is needed to have life abundantly and to share with others. Eve of the Bible was constantly called the enemy of Adam. But so was this Eve on her journey. When calling someone else your enemy, what is really being said is: "You are in-a-me" a true conscious statement from the ego. The ego does not want out of the life of its survivor, so it will cause one to think it has been mistreated and bring on war. This keeps the ego alive and kicking. The only thing Eve needs to be saved from is her lower self, the "ego," the illusion of being a victim. It is not rewarding to sign up for what you don't want to take part in.

Eve did admit that the teacher showed up in her life in so many ways and even spoke to her what she prayed he would hear for himself. LOVE YOURSELF! he proclaimed. After all what we attract is one with us. Get the message.

The perfect man, returned to his former love, Eve returned to hers. HerSELF. I am aware that we all at some point must return over and over again until the last turn becomes our Perfect SELF.

Adam was Eve's guru for knowing that nothing is ever lost, just misplaced. What Eve was refusing to see of her own stuff, Adam was staring her in the face with it all the while. She can correctly say she was starring herSelf in the face all the while, from the illusion she had created as a catalyst for this happening. Thank you SELF, for making it REAL.

A fulfilled journey is the experience that brought Eve into reality. She has chosen to go with the flow of life instead of resisting it.

We can trek up and down these roads looking for Love until we find there is the "Present" in each moment of our lives. Getting paralyzed in a life's puzzling moment only prolongs the simplicity of the truth about life. When we can live each moment in shear joy and laugh at the "ugliest", life becomes one long moment of blissful events.

We must take nothing for the insight of a journey to the place where it all began and while being there, learning Herstory. Even the insight of how much one must prepare for such a journey of leaving one destination in life in flight to another and for leaving one mind consciousness to another. The preparation for any cultural shock, adjustments, and maintenance of survival is a transformational knowledge in its self. The journey to the continent of Africa was not a small thing. This was a literal journey to a land on the same planet but of distance stretches far away by land and sea, even by the ships that sail the sky. This journey was an important one in that it was so very urgent to set foot on a place heard of but not directly experienced. Being told that the ancestors there never knew America and knowing that many trekked to what is called America today don't know about Africa. Herstory, which has been the Mystery, is yet to be told and lived in its original entirety. As the ancient saying: "The head shall become the tail," What goes around comes around" and "What was first shall be last!"

The story of THE GARDEN OF EVE

Eve was returning to an old civilization with the new found love of her heart. Instead of the time being turned forward, it was turned back. The Love in her heart was accompanied by profound pain and wonderment. In a secret chamber of her mind, this trip was to be her honeymoon, but Adam had left his hidden honey behind while in the glow of the Gracious Mother Moon could Eve find her healing balm. Eve thought she was returning to the Garden to stay forever. Little did she know that she had to go back the way she came, through hell, to erase the pain.

As she laid in the Great Moon light on the eve of their arrival to the land, upon a wet pillow from her tears, she began to pray that her journey be smooth. She woke up to thoughts of making choices based on a sound, healthy mind, body and soul relationship with Adam. Because of his anger with leaving his past love, he could not be true to Eve. Eve was not concerned with the consequences that would follow, just wanted to live in the moments she thought were sober. Eve and Adam did have some precious moments prior to their return to the garden. She chose not to remember where there is "good," there is also "evil." "Like Yin and Yang." To function in life with this knowledge one must learn to be even minded of what goes on around them. It is the choices she made that gave her experiences to elevate into a consciousness of oneness with her Creator.

We must be ready for what is ask for in life, because surly it shall come to pass. Recall asking for something and then wanting to resend it? "Sorry, I dialed the wrong number. I'll redial again."

Part I

"The Journey"

It was an encounter of an unusual kind that seemed irresistible, uncontrollable, and paralyzing. An exalted kind of love, it appeared to be.

Eve was leaving a religious event and as she was approaching her parked vehicle, a man drove up beside her, who was obviously leaving the same gathering. The driver was very handsome, inquiring about tickets to a very large event. Eve and the members in the other vehicles were selling tickets for this great event coming up soon. A mesmerized moment occurred. "Hello," my name is Adam," Well he did inform her that Hell was low from the get go. "Does anyone have tickets to the program on this coming weekend?" He spoke with his eyes fixed on Eve. It seemed the guy in the ride next to Eve heard him and eagerly dashed to make the sale but Eve reached his car first. "Greetings, I have tickets, how many would you like?" His eyes glowed and he grinned eagerly. She knew she was looking and smelling "righteously beautiful" because she was a "spiritual and physical born again "virgin" sister. She had 7 years on her celibacy. This is what seven years of living by a patriarchal religion run by "righteous men" and being in her prime age of 50 bought her. Eve was authentically beautiful. Many of the young and older brotherhood had approached her, but she waited seven years for this occasion. She had 50% joined a movement that she came to KNOW as extremely suppressive to it's female attendance. Even she was not allowed to present her God given artistic creativity talents without the competition of a brother outside the sect.

Eve asked the man, "How many tickets would you like to purchase, sir?" "I would like to purchase one for myself and one for you if I could have the honor to escorting you." This was the time that Eve thought he was sent as a test, or he was God sent. She secretly waited. He was a bit older, handsome, and seemingly on the same path as she. Eve felt he had something up his sleeve though. "Oh, you would like to escort me to the concert. That could be possible. Look I am in a hurry to join some of the members for lunch and we are driving there now." "Would you mind if I join you and I could get the tickets from you there? Eve nicely said, "Well sure, you are welcome, you can follow me there." Eve looked in her rear view mirror to see if he was keeping up with her and he was right there on her tail. And after seating and looking over the menu, he asked, "May I treat you?" "No, thank you." He insisted.

Eve motioned for a sister friend to come sit with them and witness the beginning of what became a truly unsuspecting development. At least she didn't see it coming.

He shortly became a part of the group as well, going through the conversion of a new way of life, it seemed, and his learned intelligence was very impressive in "deeds" to the "in control" members of the organization. He was very knowledgeable and helpful in all that he offered to do. The higher ups seemed to be very impressed. Eve gathered with many of the other sisters who observed that he had other motives in mind. Occasionally someone will come right into an organization and roll their sleeves up and plow right in only to have a motive of walking out with something or someone for their personal benefit. Or they could come and lay down a stack of green every now and then and become a member of a higher up order of the religion. The higher ups smoked this out before Eve did and watched to see where this was going. She refused being bate with her beauty and charm to be later auctioned off underhandedly to the best man as the ideal virtuous woman.

The ideal virtuous woman will cook, sew, and maybe sing and dance and she will have as many babies as she can, if she can. Having babies was not an option for me. In this patriarchal domineering cult the "sister" has a good chance of getting a "brother" if she had some form of assets like a "good job", house, or property. The sisters and brothers are encouraged to go over seas to the bigger compound where there are more "brothers" and "sisters" available for families. These religions allow men to have more than one wife while the woman is only allowed one husband. But what woman in her healthy mind would want that much multiple energy unless the energy was identical. Could this be why their God is call "He" and "Him"? Or could they know that the Female is both male and female. A woman in this type of organization will easily fall into this entrapment hook, line and sinker when she is desperate for a family. She will even defend the logic of the organization. Eve was about to be kicked out anyway after making "sisterhood" because she was witnessing what would not allow her to be her Goddess Self. Eve was told that she could be nothing without a man. That she was created from his rib. WOW!

Well Eve chose her man (manifestation) companion and the organization will probably make an example of her that she did not follow the laws (made by man, written in a book translated by man and taught by man) and therefore she was punished, even by mannish women.

Eve realizes she came to know her Goddess Self through the religion regardless of its patriarchal standards and she is grateful that she made the choices she did in the long run. The woman will never know and exude her Goddesshood in a patriarchal religion. She will always be "sister", a non powerful nun, in the name of the "Father." Her mother is no where to be found, unless she is also one of the "sisters."

Time had spiraled to where Eve and Adam became more than brother and sister, more than friends and beyond (low and behold against all the rules), they became husband and wife. This is against the "way" of the organization.

Eve spent seven years in celibacy of offering her sacred womb for marriage. She accepted the idea to be a "virgin" or being a celibate woman, made her a "Holy" woman. (Not knowing she was already a Whole Woman.) She hid behind the fig leaf shame to be intimate with the man she thought she loved. She found that he was celebrating his seventh year of sobriety to firewater (alcohol). He then blamed Eve for breaking that sobriety when it was the organization that produced the intoxicating beverage that he kept communion with occasionally. The short lived marriage began to descend as well as his irresponsible choices. "Dear, I have to travel out of town for my job and I will be gone for a few days." "All right my Love, I'll pack and make you a care package for the road, have a good safe trip honey." Eve found his trips were for pleasure and not business. It all blew up in her face. Somebody else was biting on that apple besides Eve. Bitterness set up in her mouth about the situation, but she had come too far, to go any farther. She began to have nightmares when he traveled. Her intuition was kicking in. She ignored it and kept moving on up the road. He later confessed about the ongoing affair and it was hell from that moment on.

Life had suggested Eve make this journey alone prior to meeting her Adam, but she allowed a distracted set of thoughts set her on a low road with her companion.

Prior to their meeting, Eve was at a contented place in her life, remember the words of sisters in her circle that they felt it was time for that perfect Adam, "Mr. Right" to show up in her life. Knowing words have power, Eve was careful not to allow those words to come from her mouth, but they undoubtedly came forth through the thoughts of others for her. Thoughts certainly are things, if you don't believe that, just look around in your life's events or even in your immediate room and see did you not think of what you see right in front of you, before it was ever there. She was about the busy-ness of experiencing a new culture, its ways and how it would apply to her spiritual growth.

This culture was preparing her to "Go Home." The truth spiritually is that we are already "home" and so it is the mental aspect of ourselves that must be transformed to realize the at-one-met (atonement) with The Divine Creation and thus we become complete physically through coming into harmony with our spiritual nature that we arrive home.

And so, Adam and Eve struggled with this marriage to save it or to tare it down and go on about their way. They made their move on to Africa. Eve was very sad most of the time. The hurt of the deception of another woman and leaving the family and friends she knew truly loved her, this way was unbearable. This should have been enough to warn her that he had a serious problem. This is the typical addictive behavior to dictate and control another and make the other person to think they are the ones with the problem. And we do take on the addictive behavior without the use of the substance.

Eve longed for her mother's nurturing. She had fallen and there was no hand to pick her up. Only hands to beat her up. Eve was strong enough to know that the only God to knock her down was the one that favored men only and make example of other women should they go against men. Though, Eve couldn't see that then.

Part II

"Hold on, a change *is* coming"

Eve began to awaken. Eve watched her whole lifestyle change when she chose to allow for an exclusive relationship with this strange fellow, replacing everything that was going on in her life. This caused all those who knew her to look at her in a very different way. It was all good, this she came to know later, which is now, but it certainly didn't look to anybody, that way, back then. Her own intuition was so pronounced during this time in her life and seemed to call out for her attention but the change in my lifestyle was so drastic, Eve chose to ignore her intuitive sweet Self. Lord, (law, the law that says, "Be still and know that I AM God.") Eve sometimes tried to imagine what it really could have been like had she made other choices that day or like for one, made the choice not to make the journey to Africa or to have made it alone. It appeared that this love connection demanded all of her and none to be shared with anyone else, Eve was ready, willing and able to give him her all, as soon as she could assure her circle of family and friends that the mind of the ego was dying and the mind of God was in there for the long haul.

Religiosity is not designed to cause one to ascend spiritually but to practice a set of ways to perpetuate the motive of the patriarchal system.

It was Eve's eagerness to find her own way through this madness, although she had no clue as to the walk she was about to take in a marriage to the man she fell so in love with. Eve and Adam did have moments of fun and laughter, they both loved nature and toured many nature parks in the states, and Adam adored Eve's culinary skill for her creative meals before leaving. Upon living in Africa they would even retreat from their differences to the rain forest for any peaceful moments they could be in together. The couple would often go in seclusion of one another and then meet in the evenings to try comforting the other. Pure Love would somehow show up when they were still long enough and without the intrusion of his past.

Eve's focus was wrapped into making this relationship merge into oneness. But there was a huge gap between them. He had a hidden agenda.

One day he was so bitter and disordered that he called Eve every foul name written and made up some. He hated the sight of her. Eve asked, "Would you feel better if you spoke with her?" he responded, "Maybe." "Then go and call her since she told you that she was weeks pregnant with your child on one of those occasional business trips, as you called it. He went to make his call and returned hours later. "Well, how is she?" "She lost the baby." Eve remained calm, knowing "the plot thickens" ... He waited as they both stared into the raging ocean. "Do you believe she really was pregnant since she pulled this off once before, prior to your meeting me?" "I can only go on what she says, Eve." "Your misery has a great impact of me, but I have to release you to her." "Why now, when you wouldn't before we left America?" "I foolishly needed you to be with me. Now I know that is not possible." I trusted my intuition to find out what I have found today. How will I ever be after the deception of two people in my face?" We walked back to our dwelling place alone in silence with pain edging us both I'm sure. His pain was his irresponsibility to himself and to others. What was Eve to do? "Adam, I resent that I allowed myself to fall for this situation. She is very young and she feels she needs you too. I now realize why I came this far, I mean literally and I will find the way to turn around, even if I have to leave and return without you." Eve and Adam had a very long evening apart as he must have gone out drinking, the way he usually tried to cope with everything. The next morning broke and they spoke as though to continue their conversation from the words last spoken from the edges of the bed, back to back.

The pressure of this was beginning to kick in before she could be set free. Eve broke as she leaped to the floor of her bedroom that evening, with her heart racing, her mind racing and her body seeming out of control. She ran to the bar to find him again, this was night after night that she wanted to make some sense of this between them and to change their vision of this situation to how it would come to an end. The truth does come but it kicks your behind before it sets you free. Most of us choose not to be uncomfortable but what is resisted does persist.

The man who literally drove up from out of no where, was suddenly now here. It seems like it happened on the day before she was in the clearest of her mind, since the day before her coming to this earth. This man brought with him the darkness she needed to return back unto the sense she was born with. This thing with Adam came to Eve to return to herSelf and keep her EYE wide open and the other two eyes shut tight. Being open to the real-eyes-ation of a "Mr. Right" showing up in her life one day came with realizing there was a glitch of seeking external to who she really is being. Eve recalled wanting to know her father for so long and when she did, even then her sense of satisfaction was that she found the truth of the matter. It *is* the truth that makes us free.

Adam was "Mr. Right" alright. Eve gets to go pass red and continue her journey. She gets why he is there and is in the process of setting him free. She is beginning to see herself as not the actor but the one observing the action. In other words, Eve is starting to switch roles from being the Drama Queen to being The Queen watching all the drama.

Adams woman had to have had a mountain of insecurities to spend her time waiting for him after seeing you destroy a relationship that could have been his saving grace. Eve had it going on in her little world. She was very spiritual, very well liked and loved by a world of people she was involved with. He for that matter was really unknown to her until she met some of the main characters of his immediate family who were not so fond of him. He seemed to have left a trail of dust to be cleaned up of those he had disappointed in some way or another. Eve had her warnings but she always kept her head beyond the stars. There is no one like this Goddess Eve. So much chaotic changes took place moment by moment until the moments became days, weeks, months and a couple of years. She questioned her God Self, can the end become something new and wonderful?

Just then she heard words echo in my head; "Only when you turn around and go the path you were on before … Eve cried out loud as she ran screaming that night. No one seemed to hear her cry. Healing, Healing, Healing, was all she could scream for, it was becoming unbearable, and no one seemed to hear her cry. She could hardly stand another moment within miles of him. "Let me out of this burning hell!" She found the words fleeing from her mouth as she tore out running into the road to no where. The natives jetted out after her, but her legs seemed to grow inches longer as she ran. Tears flew past her like a hurry cane hurrying to find him who cut him down. She declared she had gotten all that she was to get from this journey. Her healing was coming fast. She could tell because this cry felt so good to let it finally go!

The sadness was that the man she thought she knew after a round of drinks, still said "I love you." He had no love for himself. He never remembered the night before, or the morning after and really, she knew him better now than before leaving the other land she knew so well. The real him she thought she knew never stood up. Now "Mr. Right" began to appear weak and worn, tired and torn, desperate for salvation. "I want to know peace! She cried out.

Eve became quiet as though she was actually expecting to see a change automatically in the instant moment. She was fed up. She watched as the fire dwindled to smoke. Her tears were no doubt the water that put out the fire. The raging anger going on in her heart saddened those around her. All she knew was that she had to follow through to the end. Hopefully there would be light at the end of this tunnel of lies.

For the goodness of life, the absorption of a foreign homeland was devastating and invigorating at the same time. There was no such thing as time or space for her anymore. She began to watch the movie screen roll before her eyes. A new beginning or just to be brought strength enough to fight this evil trickster walking around with a grin on it's face fooling even a old woman. Speaking the same lying line to the young women he would meet for the first time "you remind me of the daughter I always I wished I had." The last person before leaving America he spoke those words to was Eve's own daughter.

Eve's mind was calmed for a series of moments when she allowed herself to be one with the natural soul of Africa. It also seemed that the ancestry in her on soul was glad to see through her eyes where she trekked across the globe. Many of those she knew had become strangers to the heated part of the world and there she found those on that continent were also Africans who never found out where their descendants went from them. Eve's desire is to bring this education to those who want to know. This part of the world is so sweet in all its giving and nurturing. Eve's African spiritual brother raised her all over again with the spirit of Africa, (the land of Ra, the Father Sun's so snug against his people's face) with pride in its genuine sense. From beholding an elder woman walking in the hottest of the day revealing her bare sagging breast after she had fed the whole village, a woman carrying a baby in her belly, on her back, by hand on each side *and a* bucket of water on her head as she strolled gracefully through the town. Eve witnessed the most unusual group of six young teen girls sitting in a circle braiding each others hair. Families all out in the yard having their supper from their laps while chickens and goats roam free, bothering no one.

Watching markets of fresh food sold daily from the fresh ripened harvest and an elder man sitting on the ground for the longest time cleaning his teeth with a chew stick was fascinating. Children running and laughing as they played with sticks and stones and most exotic plants and flowers with vivid colors that were healing just to look at and seeing a bug walking on the road that was obviously first cousin to the same bug found in the homes of America, the roach.

The Sun land is a place where Love and Respect is in tact. This filled Eve's heart with gladness as this fallen luv had filled her heart now rising in love herself all over again. But with sadness, she could not help wondering would he ever get the chance to feel what she was beginning to feel.

"Falling in love" is greatly sung about and has made the music industry billions of dollars, while the one falling in love soon meets pain. People sing to songs with lyrics such as; "I'm Falling In Love, wanting it to be forever," "I think I'm falling in Love" I say, if you think you are falling, don't you want to brace yourself or yell for someone to catch you before you hurt yourself? Most people do and getting up is not an easy thing to do. Well, It's true, this thing called love has so many meanings that Eve wondered if the lyricists knows the difference. She fell and almost couldn't get up and getting up was painful.

Eve spent ninety days in this paradise, attaching herself to a stranger making him baggage she finally left behind literally. Only then my focus became clear. Not bombarded by confusion, deceit, plotted lies and cowardliness. Days showed as days in paradise with "her love." Where was the Love for myself?

When there were moments that the ocean's roar captured my attention, the great Self of Eve would whisper deep into my ears right in the midst of a hellified moment that everything was in perfect order, Just ride with the tide maybe everything will come our just fine.

Eve began to see how she had blurredly compromised her own spiritual habits because of the blocks she allowed to test the foundation she walked upon. Not the religion, but the Spiritual nature that dwelled within.

It had come to the final day of this journey that Eve would be completing the cycle heading to where she started out from. Feelings were so scrambled, Eve knew nothing. She was numb all over from the fall and his hands that she wanted so much to reach for her were reaching for someone else. Eve finally took the hands that were always reaching out for her and pulled herself up. She returned to the Love she knew within.

Purification of the Garden … On what seemed to have been the hottest day in all of in Africa, from the beginning of the Nile River all the way up to Kuwait, Eve literally set out to walk that day to have her final thoughts put in order. For miles she walked by herself, in her own shoes this time, driven by a will, not of her own, but with a strong will that came from somewhere inside. She was not looking for someone to fall from the sky to save her. She always knew that her saving grace would come from within. It was her Spiritual Self that was to descend upon this ego to integrate with her soul. For the first half mile, her chest felt as though it had a cold cement block tied to it as she struggled to walk, while she tried to hold back tears this time but by a mile or so she couldn't any more. Just one look into a small child's eyes who looked up at her and asked in his accent but in English, "Are you hurting Madam?" Eve began to cry buckets of tears from her soul inwardly and outwardly, knowing she was trying to handle something she did not think she was going to come out of sanely or alive for that matter.

After a while, Eve could not remember how long or what distance she had come because nothing looked familiar anymore.

Eve thought she had walked into another country or possibly drifted back on planet Mars for a moment. She felt she was the only one on earth. Her tears would come and go. The fleeting thoughts of her ancestors coming to be with her would come and go also.

After walking until her shoes tore from her feet, the ground was so hot, she no longer could feel the heat. Eve was walking at a moderate pace, through an unfamiliar place, while in her heart, she knew no peace, Eve began to pray out loud as she walked; "Oh Mother, please let this anguish cease! I am leaving with an unfulfilled journey and I just want to live in joy for the rest of my days. I didn't really want to leave here, there was another purpose for my coming, but the perplexity of this man has been all in my ears. Oh' Great Mother please hear my prayer." Eve was really somewhere else in her mind. She didn't know how she was going to leave him. While Eve continued her walk she felt a sense of ease, then the further she got she felt the rushing breeze of the palm trees from the oceans roar.

The further Eve walked she began to not notice herself anymore. First, went the feelings from her feet, her legs, then her arms, her heart, her body, and then her total self was gone. Eve was to return to America in a few days and didn't want her children to sense anything but good vibrations. Eve reckoned with herself as she walked and admitted that she will remember to honor herself first in all choices and decisions she chose ever in her life.

Eve began to speak out loud as though to dialog with a spirit of some kind, like a guardian angle. "Oh Great Ancestral Mothers, I feel you walking with me on this path right now, I feel as though you have lifted my legs and placed me where you really want me to be once again. It is as being a sleeping baby in your nurturing arms again. The feeling I believe we all long for. Oh I hope he feels this for himself right now, Oh Great Mothers." Eve began to sense the out stretched arms through the people all around her, praying, wishing her well as she walked these miles in the arms of her loving ancestors. Some of them she seemed to recognize. Her mind is beginning to float above. She began to leave all her worries and concerns to blow away by the palm trees into the ocean. "I now know that my new vision has become yours my Great Mothers, for me and all those concerned." She spoke with a smile.

"Oh Great Mothers it must be your breath pushing against my face as though I am flying or being forced through the air in an uncovered elevator. I have had this dream many times in my life." She thought. I will close my eyes now and relish the comfort of your arms as I lay … my … head … upon … your … bosom …

Eve had gone into a deep meditation, sitting under an umbrella at the beach. She was being reset to know that all was safe and well with the situation and peace was always with her. Eve began to feel her body as she was returning to her conscious thoughts of where she was and who she was. With the sense of being washed clean after leaving the estate where she lived, Eve was now given a new mind.

Eve gave thanks out loud for her rejuvenation and the energy to go on, no matter what. She was comfortably caressed and kissed to dear life in the warmth of the father sun and within a time and space that no one can define. What could have been a giant fan of cool tropical pineapple, mango, coconut breath fanned her body with the relaxation of being cried out and sweetly surrendered to whatever there was that truly loved her. It is Love yearning for its on Self. That's all. With that, she whispered gently to herself, "Thank you, Thank you, Thank you." While softly she smiled, she lays still until the evening sun set and tenderly whispered once again, "You're All Right."

Eve began to dialogue with her Higher Self Again. "For that "waking up" moment, it seemed like a life time. Eve felt herself gently and very slowly open her eyes to find that she could see what she had never seen before. She saw the most gorgeous people, beautifully shaped palm trees, the pristine sand in the most fertile land. She saw Love. Her hearing was crystal clear. The ocean called out her name and splashed her with grand oblation. The Goddess of Sacred Waters sent her a song from the whales. She heard musical Love. The Sun pierced her being with its warm blanket and laced her entire body with the kiss of Daddy Sun. Eve spoke "I know Love. Even my sense of smell is profound as I inhaled the merchant's incent of frank and myrrh. I smell Love and with a sip of sweet coconut water, I will make the sacred toast to eternal Love."

Eve consciously felt the cool sand between her toes as she sensed her motion of walking again, across the ocean's shoreline back to her estate that what seemed to be miles and miles of walking were only minutes away. She knew all was perfect and Life could never be more precious.

Eve sat again on the sand to watch the final tip of the sun go out of sight, when she almost jerked her head off to see who had just quickly planted a kiss on my cheek. She quickly blurted out "Who are you?" It was the little boy who lived next door and who so timely and so sweetly dropped her favorite fruit, a perfectly yellow ripened mango on her lap. He ran on up the beach, looking back as he waved yelling "Madame, everything is to be Alright." Eve was at that time only five minutes away from home. With that same assurance Eve had a déjàvu of her own son planting a kiss upon her cheek when leaving the America's airport with Adam for the journey and waving until he was out of sight with a yell that "Everything is to be Alright."

Yes, it's what is Real. Some call it a Miracle. We all have them and sometimes we just take them for granted. All throughout Life the Masters and Sages remind us of the "Present" that is pre-sent before. It is by thought, words, and actions that those seeds deliver the harvest.

Eve returned to her home in her own land and in the land of her own heart.

The Art of RISING IN LOVE vs FALLING IN LOVE

I know Love when there is no trace of opposition to Peace, in me and as me. Love falls out of sight where there is no awareness of Peace pervading my universe. The Perfect One does exist. I AM therefore YOU ARE too. We draw the experience that mirrors us, at the time that we draw them. It shows up when and where our soul wills it to, for the experience we need to know to recall Love just IS. Love is us willing to be known. Understanding the art of Rising in love, you'll think twice before falling in love.

We have such a vivid fantasy of how love is supposed to look and feel. We call it "romance" which is fantasy, a story, not real. It is no wonder that the question has forever been "What is Love?" With as many answers given, we are left to ponder the answer that "Love just is …" But strangely enough, we don't hear the question "Who is Love." Scores of music, movies, poems, plays, etc. have been produced around falling in love. We are told that "GOD is love". I don't really think that man believes in what he cannot see. After all man was never really taught to believe in himself who he can see, even in each other. Can one say that he is in love with God, whether he is rising or falling? Who can put a finger on love. What is Unconditional Love? Can one rise and fall in Unconditional Love? Can one really love what one cannot see that is external to oneself, whether it be a Spirit, A ghost, or a Holy Ghost?

In the meantime we keep on falling deep and rising in love. Over and over in numerous relationships, yet we never seemed to be content in love. We make such statements such as:

"I love my car.", "I love my husband.", "I love my child", "I love my dog" and "I Love nature." Are those different or various degrees of love? If so, how did love get degreed? There are overrated symbols of Love. Love is equated with money (for the love of it), health (love sickness), even sex (if you love me) Holidays (buying love). What's chocolate got to do with it? Love is attached to so many emotionally displayed actions.

I created two alternative words for the word "romance" one is AURA-MANTRA, meaning: a blissful vibration given out by a person creating a drawing power, causing those around to enjoy being in the presence of the person. The second one is AURAMANTRICKS, meaning a manipulative method for luring love actions for personal illusion of false fulfillment.

It is the aura that we sense of another. "Auramantra" feelings cause one to feel light and free. Opposite that is the "ego" creating need for attachment, conditions, promises and expectation. Our interpretation of love is unlimited and varies from one person to the next. We speak of what love is and what love is not. Some say love hurts, some feel that love feels good and even heals and some say one must be IN love.

The word FALLING means: dropping, collapsing, descending, plunging, sinking, subsiding, toppling and decreasing. The definitions are not all negative, it is just what it is, but is that what we want in Love? Love enveloped in any of these attributes could not be life giving. A fallen love belongs to someone who has fallen in their own understanding of giving, receiving, serving and being served. Those who fall in love also speak of falling out of love. Almost like rolling in and out of bed. What would constitute one falling in and out of Love except they manipulate one another with expectations and some form of conditional contract? When the fall is so hard, usually one promises to never fall in love again. I respect the beloved artist Tina Turner who sang the words: "What's Love Got to do With It?" I am sure she knows what Love really is.

The word RISING means: to ascend, climb, move upward, to mount up on wings like an eagle and soar the endless heights of forever. This is an enlivening, electrifying and elevating experience. When we are clear of who and what we are as Absolute Supreme Being in physical flesh, blood and bones then our lives will express freely and allow others the same freedom without fear of loosing anything and with no ownership of one another like a piece of land. We acknowledge the freedom space to be what the other wishes to be and offer to enhance that for the other. This is the purpose for partners. There is not much to say on Rising because the action will speak for it self. The greatest rise to me is the rise in a mother's womb as she is expecting another great idea to manifest in life's expression.

It is Love that we find ourselves, complete and whole. Love is sufficient. Love creates all that is good. That is you who read these words.

Seeing Straight

Seeing straight means single minded and focused. Notice when it seems a long time coming, the focus factor gets out of whack. We go stand out on the curb to see if what we are waiting for is far or near. When seeing straight, there is no curve. There is no hold up, there is just crooked vision. If you can't see the forest for the trees, look straight beyond the trees, the forest is right there and more. When I sit at the Atlantic Ocean on Hilton Head's Island beach, I look straight across the ocean onto the shores of Ghana and see into the city clean on into my friends houses, I can see and hear them talking. Of course, if there is something that is not my business, I see straight beyond that. I keep looking until I see straight into what I intend to see with my mind's eye. That is what I call seeing straight. There is a time for checking our vision for what we can see or what we believe to see. Believing is not seeing. Knowing is. When we can truly see with focused vision then the time for manifestation is quick. Seeing straight cuts right on through to where it is the soul longs to be. What we enjoy doing most that is peaceful, joyful and service is creatively expressing the SELF. Now that is seeing straight because the focus is on the peace, the joy and the service and not the attached results.

I am sure there is in each of us that certain special experience we have to express. A focused vision will lead right to it. If it is not in creation, we have the power to create it just from our own imagination. Just also keep within your focus that we individually are the creator as a whole. Like the spilled water is one with the water left in the glass. So is the water in the physical body to the water in the ocean.

Check the vision. Is what we imagined showing up in our lives exactly the way we saw it before it arrived? Even if it is what you did not want, did you see it coming? You know we sometimes hear ourselves saying "I knew it was coming." "I told you so." We are such creative beings that we create what we don't want better than we create what we do want. How straight is that seeing? We have the power to improve our manifestation. If we are doing it, then don't complain. It just means we are becoming more creative and our vision is becoming perfect. We can only see straight for ourselves and create for ourselves.

When we feel ourselves getting side tracked, we will know to be true by the alternate route we have to take and the delay in the vision. Discomfort is a sign that we have or are about to capsize or have gone a little to the left or a little too far to the right. It's okay though, because sooner or later we began to make adjustments in our vision and life becomes focused once again. We can see the way we were headed in the first place.

The road gets long and winding sometimes, and this is the time to know that although there are bends in the road, when remaining focused on what it is we are aiming for, the vision is not lost at all. The bend is our doubt or weariness that what we see is not a reality or deserving. This is the lack of knowing that the bend straightens by your seeing straight into where you intend to be.

I find meditation allows for going beyond the physical body into a spiritual realm that will bring the vision up close and so called "time" seems to not be a factor. Who we are knows no limits and has a strong desire to express. Sit still in nature and focus on all that is in creation and know again that the body can do what our words and mind commands it to, through the minds eye sight. There is a very good friend of mine who had a cyst removed from his back and became paralyzed from waist down. The doctors told him he would never walk again. With the power of his imagination, he visualized himself exercising everyday until he began to move his legs, then he saw himself walking, now he drives himself cross country and goes to the gym everyday. He sees straight through the bend in the road to where he intends to get and gets there. What we see and touch is a creation of our own imagination, thoughts, visualization, words, intention, action and will. Remember to focus on the goal, keep seeing straight ahead with Divine Purpose and Vision. We find ourselves where our focus is. If I make it sound simple, it is because it is. I don't know what fishermen think about out there on that dock all night, but I am sure they can just see that fish dangling off that line. If they come home with nothing, their minds might have drifted and that is all right too. Relaxation is a wonderful thing.

I found that when I keep my eyes on the road and allow no distractions, which sometimes may come, I experience smooth sailing. Just remember to keep seeing straight and you will reach your destination.

Seeing straight will allow others to see their way around to making a difference to masses of people. I admire and adore Oprah Winfrey. People like Oprah and Tyler Perry are perfect examples of someone who can see straight, in spite of the obstacles that have come. And there are many, many others who can see and are going straight to the finish line. That is a Great sign. If and when one can all can.

In my walk on this road, I sometimes think I have arrived when suddenly there comes a bend in the road. After so many of them all I do is recall the many bends I consciously saw straight through to where I am now and I keep going straight ahead.

When the road seems to have rolling hills, just roll with them as long as you can see where you are going. This is good exercise. An opportunity for meditating, contemplating and seeing what you can't see with the necked eye. Keep seeing straight. Extend those lens and see the end results if you will. The downs are beneficial where we have the opportunity to get off and get onto another road that will take us where we intent to be, go there. Some are not willing to walk on those roads. When we are willing to walk them all, we see for ourselves, we will know for ourselves that all is of the whole. To resist is to fear the unknown. To know is to surrender. Use faith with action. That is the magic to being, doing and having what you will. The ultimate to being, doing and having is the knowledge of our great Self.

All roads will eventually get you where you are going and there is no rush. Trying to speed up and go around or push others off the road is foolish. It is that the more you see on the way, the more you will know of your self. Even when you are seeing straight, in your peripheral vision you will see the beauty of your journey and the not so beauty, but in seeing straight, you will not get distracted.

One of my most favorite nursery rhymes, until this very precious moment is:

"Row, Row, Row your Boat, Gently Down the Stream, Merrily, Merrily, Merrily, Merrily, Life Is but A Dream."

It simply means for me, to allow myself to glide through the stream of life without resistance and wake up as the dreamer.

Wake Up! Life really is Great, when you are seeing straight.

Mama Nature

Spring, Resurrection is the meaning of part of the expression "Avivah." and Fall season is my most favorite time of the year, living in America. Fall is when I feel closest to nature because it is when nature begins to shed Her beautiful clothing as they crumble to the ground, releasing any fruit left in preparation for undergoing a serious transformation through winter, until spring again. After She changes her many colors, She vanishes into a slumber never turning off Her power and dreams of another cycle in Her nature. Naked and submissive to change, She is born again with numerous sunbursts and moon glows upon Her face of Glory.

"Naked She comes and naked She goes as humankind tries to mimic the color patterns of her garment. Nature has no problem yielding to the Absolute Intelligence. She is forever one with the creator, therefore always on purpose. There is no sadness in Her transformation only exhilarating resurrection to be revealed. Let your words be; I Am Resurrection. I Am Mama Nature.

Situations can and will transform from its appearance to that of something totally unexpected. Depending on where we are in our rise, will we know when the end of a situation is blessing us or leaving us to grow further in our endeavor to enlightenment? Yet In many marriage ceremonies, we were told that a marriage must be kept together "until death do us part." From past experiences, I interpret this to mean death of the marriage. Not necessarily death to an individual because death symbolizes change and not ending. To be able and willing to let go is to reach for something new. When a marriage is put together by ignorance,(ignoring the truth) of what is in harmony with the nature of our destiny, changes will come to correct it all. That is the way of Mama Nature. A friend once told me that "the purpose for relationships is to raise each other up in consciousness and purpose in support of growth." As we change, our surroundings change.

When a situation ends because of incompatibility, it sometimes indicates someone resisting the Truth and holding fast to the blind side of the road or one ascending and the other holding back. There can only be beginnings and more beginnings because there is no end to the end. That is what is meant by life everlasting. Nature knows this and so She keeps on doing what she always does best. I look forward to Her beautiful wardrobe year after year. It just goes on and on and on in some way, shape, fashion or form. Enjoy Life!

Questions often asked and answers often given.

What Is Love? "Love just is ...

What Is Death? "Death just is ... changing from one creation to another one."

What Is Life? "Life is Endless Existence."

What is Purpose? "Purpose is that which you are aiming to reach."

Living on Purpose

Living on Purpose is the BALM. Dis-order becomes Order. Living on Purpose, knowing full well what we are doing from moment to moment, consciously experiencing the moment as the "Present" we give ourselves, opens up a reality that makes us Free to be who we are. This opportunity is given to us for our inner "in" joyment. Past, present and future are great paradigms of the moment.

Being clear about what and why we do what we do, we recognize those who are walking around in a daze seeking to KNOW or to WAKE up! Many of us have been there and done that, so we can relate and smile and know, that's on purpose as well.

Life itself is on purpose and everything about it. In our striving we all will come to know that we can live on purpose continuously.

We begin to attract those whose purpose is connected to ours and we become supportive to one another. Our purpose being connected is then being lived up in a "Let Us get it done together" "One for all, All for one" attitude, and our moment to moment experiences in life become a oneness, without attachment. It has to be without attachment.

It is the imperfect that needs Love. There is a need to be needed. The perfect already is complete and is Love. We will experience being The Great Cosmic Mother, in the flesh, once we get beyond seeking. There is where our purpose is known and fulfillment is ever fulfilling. Perfection needs no attention, acknowledgment. Open the "Present" moment by moment. The "Present" holds contentment for it is the ultimate of life, as long as there is no attachment to it. When there is willingness to release that present, we allow for the next one. Many motivational coaches have dis-covered that truth from our own personal experiences.

Remember any bumps, tosses or turn arounds are experienced when we are not on purpose or seeing straight. No experiences are good, bad, right, wrong, better or worse, they are simply opportunities to look at the situation another way. It is a waste of time and energy giving them judgment when experience is there to set you straight. Grow from it. Develop a habit to complete any project that is started on purpose, so that in each moments "Present" you are clear of its intent. To procrastinate is to put off. Prolonging the experience of knowing the purpose is depriving others of what you came to express that will make a difference in life. Why do we do that? I say because we don't get a sense of urgency about what purpose is. We just want to be comfortable in life. Yet the question is always lurking on our minds. Just remember PURPOSE IS DIRECTION. When you know your purpose, you also are clear of your direction. Purpose is your compass to arrive into YOURSELF, HOME. There is no place like Home.

Many times we go through life asking questions about our purpose for being, but the answer lies within the question. Just give it time and you will know who, what, why, where and when of the purpose is to show up. Ask yourself what is it that you love doing more than anything in the world and is it something that would enlighten others and lead them to the wholeness of their being. What are the compliments you get for being who you are? Look at how you can express that something to make a contribution to life. To do something on purpose is to do it with the intention of being the example of Truth, Love, Peace, and Order.

I Am You

This writing I leave with you in good faith. I can't say enough about that "present." Within each breath of life is the moment of a great "Present," given unto us to open. We can be thankful for every "Present" that we keep coming through, in each new breath of life. Joy comes from our focus on opening each new "Present" in each new moment. We are taken care of just by knowing that the Gift of Life is breathing in our "Present".

A Pyramid/Christmas tree of Truth

I wish you merry consciousness all year round.

Identify your greatest mountains in life, then rise, rise, rise above them.

Identifying your greatest mountains in life will assist you in rising above them and looking at where you have been in areas of your life. The areas you express in work, talent, with people, with the planet, is the walk you choose as you ascend in the direction of dis-covering who you are.

Be absolutely honest in reaching back as far as you can in your life mystery, mystory, history, herstory and "yourstory." Just remember that you have stories but you are not them. They are just experiences we impressed with to be expressed as more comes. Our Stories are stored up expressions. So share them if you will.

Make a list of mountains you've climbed, entitling and approximately dating them individually, then write the experience, the outcome and the wisdom you received that healed you. Choosing to make them brief for your own purpose will allow you to list as many as you possibly will. When you are healed and free, you may want to share them with those close to you or those youths you wish to prevent the climb of those mountains and bring healing to them as well. As one of my close brothers said once, the word "Miracle" really means "Me as the oracle." We become the enfoldment of our own destiny. We are the dreamer, so awaken and meet the real Self.

There is an awesome ancient legend of a bird that flies forward with its head and long neck delicately turned looking backwards. The legend has many interpretations. I interpret it to mean that, in order to move forward one must remember from whence he came and be conscious of what has learned from those previous experiences no matter how far back they go. Sankofa moments assist in being in the moment as we create what is thought to be the future. The truth is, the past and the future both exist in this very moment.

In keeping a journal of Sankofa moments will give us the advantage of peeping into our patterns and making any changes to clearly be creatively effective to your conscious desire. Being conscious keeps us free. Being unconscious is blinding.

It is rewarding to personally journal, date, and log at the end of your day the upside and the downside of our experiences.

1. Special Love treatment, I gave myself today.
2. Victory experienced today.
3. Unpleasant experience today.
4. The way I handled my day.
5. What awakening I discovered today.
6. Goal worked on today.
7. My awareness today.

Ancestral Arts

My Auntie practiced Voudun in a sacred and beautiful way. She often said: "Never wish for others that which you would never want for yourself, because it will come back to haunt you." she also said, "Those who do, are ignorant of the ancestral laws and their ignorance is certainly no excuse from the consequence. You must always seek to do right by others. No matter how much they offer you, tell them you don't do no dirty work, because it will back fire not only on them but on you as well. You can't intervene on someone else's life path because it is not up to you to change the course. Only yours can you change. Even their belief or non belief has no ties on their life. Only what they know will determine their own destiny." Auntie passed that knowledge on to me as though she thought I would need it.

My grandmother said to me once, "Seek to remove the compulsion to allow anger swell within you for that temperament will bring harm to yourself and to those you feel anger for. You must learn to be confident in yourself and your loved ones, that in knowing who you are and that you are the protection you desire, there is nothing to be protected from."

An unwise use of the arts will cause his or her consequences by not using wisdom. The ultimate use of the great Ancestral Arts is in the hands of the Gods and Goddesses who know they are. Rituals are performed by everyone. We may not know that we perform daily rituals but they are actions we have programmed to bring us certain results. When actions are purposely done for the desired results and done with certain paraphernalia such as purified water for libation, dressed candles, incense, sounds of water fall, music, chants, these are what makes for a sacred ritual that invokes certain results. The results must be for the good, well being and betterment of all concerned. It is greater to know that to purify a certain space for the performance of sacred rituals for your own self is to intentionally perform them with knowledge of certain Moon positions. This is in harmony with the energy of the planets as we are all connected by the vibration of the zodiac, whether we know it or not. Ritual must be performed daily to the Goddess and to keep her symbols at hand keeps a window open for Her guidance.

I do not know everyone in the world by name, but to visualize world peace and wellbeing for all and keep a focused and pure mind eventually this realization will be known to all at a divine appointed time. This is the focus of all Masters, the desire of our great ancestors and genuine leaders. When the concern is for more than self, more power is placed upon the wonderful results.

In my family lineage of Ancestral Arts, life has shown sacrifices that the women who have come through tragic experiences had to endure to break a curse to be lifted for an eternal fortress of security in mind body and soul. With the birth of the last female of this millennium to this line of females, that sacrifice was lifted with an eternal fortress of security. This female is and will forever be the Goddess of Life in the flesh and keep order where there is nobility. She will be known at the summit of her Love Life.

While ever discovering the height of The Great Cosmic Mothering power, I am grateful and humbly welcome all the greatness to come. It is urgent that the Female seriously comes to know her true inherent Self. She is breath. Without her there is no life. Just to know this is the consent to have life free of any degree of pain. This is Ancestral Art.

Let Us Make Man Undivided

◆

(Written for a Narrated Performance)

The beginning reader is a strong, baritone male voice.

Male Narrator:

"There is no beginning." The Matriarchal Soul-Onyx, The Great Cosmic Mother God of Divine Darkness created HerSelf from the deep and dark consciousness of HerSelf out of The Divine Embryonic waters of Her Divine mind.

The Great Cosmic Mother God swam by her own umbilical connection to all that was to be of HerSelf, by HerSelf. She arose from the great waters of Her essential organism, the embryonic ocean, the water of all life. The Great Cosmic Mother God gave birth to MATTER.

For a long span of time, She nurtured Her Divine Creation for total compatibility to life Flawlessly. Yes, in a language we all can comprehend, life is of a Divine Cosmic Feminine Fabrication. She gave birth and nurturing unto HerSelf that Her total Cosmos be fulfilled abundantly and in Divine Cosmic Order.

Today Man poses the question: "Which came first, the chicken or the egg?" They came as one conception. She released the egg to its Divine Darkness in the cosmic ocean for its Divine time of appearance.

The Great Mother basked in the Soma glow Her cosmos moon light. The light of HerSelf illumined so much, that Her thoughts pressed out Her desire for infinite expansion. As She began to dilate centimeters of infinity, there was HerSelf duplicated throughout Her creation. Goddesses begot themselves for eons of cosmic time. Their birthing ground grew energy and space with the most sacred places throughout in a universe of both physical and spiritual energy. World of worlds will orbit in the whirl of the breath of The Great Cosmic Mother.

Ancient impenetrable monuments pay tribute to Her being and are found all around this earth as we know it today. In the universe reflecting Her Highness, Her Wonderment, Her statue of embodiment and Her Powerful multitudes of existence, She documented HerSelf upon the earth, with legend, until She would

Rise with flesh. She is the creator of Divine Language. The language spoken to plant life, animal life, foul and mammal, her closest likeness in flesh, in flight, in the movement of the waters, even the water houses the Breath of the Great Mother, as Her voice echoes silently, under the water, musical ecstasy into the nights of infinity. Man today wonders the great cry of the whales as She moves upon the waters still to make known her Divine presence. With Her hands ripples the magic of Her beauty. The "Her maids", not mermaids tend the waters of the shores in the night and take in the devotions and rituals of children to the ancestral Mothers. Her great Crocodiles who guard the waters cut off any rituals made against her offspring upon the earth. The offering, the planting, weaving, sculpturing, sewing, dying, painting, building, designing, crafting, farming are endless facets of Her. She gives endlessly. The Great Mother is the whole cosmic system, complete with Her Divine Male Nature of protection, ever accelerating strength with the iron blade of courage. She creates HerSelf in Order to know HerSelf and to know HerSelf in the Hueman experience.

The Great Cosmic Mother has always said, "Yes, I am made in the image of MySelf." Heaven is "As Above, So Below." I am MySelf being expressed from my Heart on Earth, Cosmic Wonderment. Hidden in the words "She" you find me and in the words "Her" you find me, both male and female "In Her Chi" (energy).

Male and Female Narrators:
Make the request: Will all who choose, speak the names, in unison, of the many Great Mothers witnessed in the earth, personal and Herstorical giving thanks for allowing us to recognize Your Greatness. Let Us Be One With You.
Sound Effects:
A soft drum roll and an African cry out as the drum roll heightens and comes to a sudden halt.
Female Narrator:
"One splendid evening, after so many eons of moons and suns, The Great Cosmic Mother Goddess bestowed upon HerSelf, of Her multifaceted spirit."
Closing Scene:
The beautiful Goddesses dance into a sacred huddle.
Female Narrator: Exclaims loudly.
"WOMAN! Let Us Make Man Undivided, in our own image!"

Male Narrator:

"The Great Mother had so much divine joy with Her Selves playing in the cosmos for more than an eternity and in life's years, uncountable of man. She played in Her sacred water, in the perfectly scented fresh air beneath the glistening stars and the stillness of the precious night. The Goddesses played along the floral gardens and laced their braided hair with the floral bouquet of the earth. When they settled down in a water fall upon boulders of rocks, they lay comfortable, as the vanishing Sun kissed them another good night and the Moon glow stroked their curves and cooled their bodies in the waves of golden grain. A sleep occurred with visions of the excellence of Man in their midst. Her labor was Her sport, Her play." (There are sounds of wind and rain.)

"When they did awaken from the long and deep sleep, they embraced one another gleefully and they all immediately danced into a circle and began to gaze into the center of the Eye of all perfection. (Dancers form a circle as they moan in the pleasure of their ecstatic pregnancy's laboring joy, in preparation for their desired presentation of a greater part of creation.)

In total harmony, they all began to move in perfect motion that appeared as a golden light swirling around and around in the figure of the number eight 8. Through and throughout space in preparation for the great event, they prepared for the grand ritual. In the wonderment of the moment they all gathered in a circle.

The Great Cosmic Mother God stands up from the circle of Goddesses as they bow and kneel circling Her. (She shows Her respected for each of them with the same gesture.)

A spoken chorus of female voices: chanting: "Let Us Make Man Undivided!" And So It Shall Be, Let Us Make Man Undivided!, And So It Shall Be.

Female Narrator:

The Great Cosmic Mother God speaks: Lowly as a prayer then loudly "Let Us Make Man Undivided and In Our Own Image! Beautiful, Strong, Faithful and True, Compassionate, Confident and Masculine Too."

In same chorus female voices: A Divine Companion.

Song: Sung by Female Narrator: "A song of Femininity" written by Avivah

Female Narrator:

"He appeared right there in the midst of them as they encircled Him, by hundreds of rows. The finest thing they had ever witnessed in creation.

A charcoal black man, with the perfect anatomy of Her greatest imagination. Well built. He emerges slowly from the cosmic circle of Goddesses. (Male is of the deep dark melanin complexion standing in a frozen pose, with his hands to his heart in honor of the Undivided Mother as he turns to look at the Creation of HimSelf. Then the Female dancers will reach to the top of his head with a crown. Male begins to the dance performance)

Female Narrator:

"There stood a charcoal black Hueman, the hue that envelopes the total spectrum of color. Hue is the color that pervades the universe. Color is the sacred vibration of the Great Cosmic Mother. She is The Undivided, whose home is the Deep Darkness of The Black Onyx, Her womb."

Male begins to dance, creatively using his every muscle pronouncing his masculinity. "Umph, Umph!" He is good, and very good. His heart beats as the drums of the Mother's land. His hair is as fine as lambs wool and his body a dark copper and bronze. His eyes are of fire. He is the glorious carpet spread over the Georgia Mountains of the fall season. His melodious breath came forth as the strongest wind of ten thousands brass horns. He leaned back and exclaimed":

Male Narrator:

"Wooooomb Of Mannnnn!"

Male Narrator: Male voices began to chant OM with the deep baritone of creation. Female dancers leap with joy softly, as The Male, serenades in dance humble gratitude for his creation to 12 female dancers as male narrator sings. The 12 Goddess dancers leave the stage leaving the one female dancer as The Great Cosmic Mother God Herself. He dances with his bare skin glistening and He leaps with joy. He bows on one knee, in thanks and praise to The Great Cosmic Mother God for his creation. She stretches forth Her arms to him to nestle him upon her bosom and the Male dancer stretches his hands around Her, sliding one arm to lift her, as the 12 Goddesses come in with strands of colorful ribbons whirling around The Great Cosmic Mother God and her God as they become one.

Curtain Close:

In a stillness moment of soft drumming, the drumming gets louder.

Female Narrator:

Song is played

Song: Female Singer

Light dance, while sounds of drumming to accentuate male and female dance cohabitation

"It appeared in the twinkle of an eye from the deep embryonyx sleep (sleep within the womb) of the Great Cosmic Mother's dream, She experienced Her heart's desire. As she thinks She becomes. Being made in Her image, it is just like that. Her matriaonyxical Love is magnetically awesome. The Great Cosmic

Mother God danced Herself into a sacred trance and began to reflect Her magical and majestic powers with Her beautiful and Spiritual merrymaking. The Great Cosmic Mother God, conceives Her first born with Her first born man. Her light dance commences. She slowly rises to dance in Her embryonyx state of mind that In Her vision of dance She dances and dances until She singularly mellowed out into joy as the Man slowly began disappear from sight.

Intensifying drumming:

Male Narrator:

"Mother feels the time to breathe Divine Principle into her Magnificent Creation of Divine Companionship to establish perfect order.

Curtain Open:

The leading Male dancer appears on stage sitting beside The Great Cosmic Mother God sitting on chase lounge. The leading Male holds her hand as she appears to speak across to Him, eye to eye. He kisses both her hands and she kisses him left cheek to right cheek.

Female Narrator:

Speaking sensuously, "All creation you are now aware of is of my image. It is perfect as it is. It is yours, and ours My Beloved. My Goddess shall be heaven on earth to you and you shall rejoice and be glad in it! Play in it and have your heart's desire in it. We will be as one and many more shall come through us. I am all that you will need upon the earth. You will love, honor and adore me as your Divine Self. There is no shortage in my Goddess hood. My love for you is Infinite. We are one in the Spirit of Divine Love. We are one in GOD as GOD. We are the Generator, The Originator and the Destroyer at will. There will be peace, love and Just Us for all.

Our Soul Onyx Dance together creates more after our kind. We were before the beginning and we will forever BE.

Music with the echo of the word "Forever" whispered.

Female reader continues:

I make no mis takes and My time is the right time. You are not to entertain a false self or you will edge me out and you will become extinct by your false self."

Male dancer extended forth his arms as he swirled to embrace Her.

The Great Mother stood strong her position placing her hands above her head. As though Her spoken word is enough.

Female Narrator:

"Individually, by the power of the Great Mother she appears as one and many at the same moment of time and space."

(Male dancer dance in while each woman dances alone and bows toward him.

Man immediately reached to have his moment with one of the Goddesses, then another, then another, then another. Mother divided HerSelf to express the memory of Her multifaceted Self and She allowed man to multiply to please Her in multiple ways.

The Divine Great Mother, as she dances across the stage of life, in all Her creation of "Goddesy" there will always be Divine Order, even and especially with the birth of the man.

The Divine Mother never had to question HerSelf or Her creation.

Until!

Strong drumming: then soft drumming and music:

Male reader:

The Great Goddess Mother chose to lay down to rest and Her rest became Her sleep. She encountered the experience of a dream, that in Her dream, drums rolled soft, then loud, them soft, then loud again as Her heart beat with many attempts to awaken.

The sound of rain

A great horrific rain came. The Great Mother did not create Rain. It was the voice of the EGO. She dreamed She and her Man were making beautiful love when He was suddenly taken by the ego, The false sense of HimSelf that would now create HimSelf extinct against the will of HerSelf. He struggled to mount her and put Her beneath him. Her only desire was to give him Heaven on earth. She immediately ceased the struggle and woke HerSelf to realize She was reading His dream that He could redefine the will of the Great Cosmic Mother God and would mis taken the EGO against the will of HimSelf. He was now creating HimSelf extinct.

Male reader:

Man has strayed far away from His very own nature. His spending away by His good signature for money, power and control all for His own will soon bring him down to the ground. He bought himself the demonstration of the "ego" spirit that feeds off of an illusion of emotions of feelings, guessing, and forgetting from whence the ego came. His buying into this illusion also bought resetting his Creator's initial Creation into a retroactive combustion with chaotic times and seasons, a fulfilling of signs and prophecies. "It's not nice to fool with Mother Nature" became a smooth chant in the back of his head. The warning soon faded out as Man proceeded to edge the Goddess out.

Male reader:

"Ahhhh so you are seeking to edge God out."

Female reader:

"Nothing exists without Me, not even My dreams, not even MySelf. I cannot imagine Life without Man, for if Man dreams of Life without Me, He is no more HimSelf and His dream is gone forever, so why all this talk about he, he, he? What about the MAMA.

Male reader:

Man continued to manifest upon earth and perform against His Creator.

When the Truth became altered where in its very nature was divinely organic, a crisis alert vibrated throughout the Goddess Motherhood consciousness. Her nature went through the change of life, which meant She had to put the Men on pause for a great moment, to see just what was their trouble?

Hold On, all Ye Divine Mothers, you gave them free will and this is what happens!

Female reader:

The Original Peaceful Creation had deliberately slipped into a Patriarchal "egoin" seizure, In other words, Taken by Force! Deviation from the Truth! Man began to imprison Himself because He could no longer contain HimSelf. He had sought to make it on His own. "I don't need a Woman to tell me what to do." "If she can't take care of me, I will cease to take care of her. After all she is the Mother of my seed. Let her take care of them since she is so strong. She thinks she can be the Man and the Woman too."

Female reader:

And the woman began to follow her Mans rebellion to the Great Cosmic Mother God in her saying: "I can do badly all by myself." "I don't need a man." "I'll just seek welfare to take care of me and my children." "Look at Him, he has become a ladies man." "Oh no, he is also a man's man."

Male reader:

"Look at her, she has allowed man to make her unworthy." More and more of humanity is beginning to fade into the "ego" as The Great Cosmic Mother God allowed Her Creation to exist, there was a raging urgency.

Economic, political, chemical and every other warfare is beginning to break out on to nature. There is war on Her air, water and Her food She allows her earth's body to produce for nourishment while living upon the earth. This madness of the cows feeding on themselves and being crossbred and the creation of hybrid vegetation must stop!

Female voice of rage: as The Great Cosmic Mother.

"My nature appears to become extinct. That appearance will have to be a reality for there to be a reverse appearance. The animals, the birds and the rest of nature do not have to suffer as much as the Hueman, because of their surren-dered participation in the scheme of life. Hueman will have to experience what it has never experienced before. I gave you the medicine to prevent any ailments and I created your bodies for the experience of the earth, not to fight one another because of differences. All is the likeness of Me. Your thoughts, words and deeds are not mine when they create disharmony. They are fragments of distorted understanding of Me. Your foolishness keeps you from your hearts desire and external from that which you already are and have to be.

You count illusionary years for "birthdays" as my Earthdays go unnoticed and disregarded daily. Everyday I give to you and you have no regard for me now, even to walk on the grown in gratitude or to come and sit with your Mother and show Her the Love She has shown you. You cry and hurt because you feel unloved. Those are my feelings you feel. When you return that which you desire you are forever happy. I and I alone have the power to activate the returned Love you so desire, merely because that is what I am. You attempt to give and receive false love and that is what you get in return and you find yourself crying into your pillows. I cry when you cry, I laugh when you laugh. I am you. When my Sun beams and the dew moisten the gardens, they are both giving and receiving. Such is life. The Great Cosmic Mother endowed each and everyone the talents pos-sessed.

Female reader continues:

The Great Mother Goddess began to speak from Her sleep.

(Laying on stage under a netted veil)

"I cannot be disguised, for greatness is my aspiration. Any subtle covering of me with a veil of any kind will soon be lifted. I eventually allowed MySelf to be dropped out of sight by Man as to him I am degenerative in nature, unimportant and unworthy to be praised. Yet in a little while, through it all, the earth will come to remember and know me again as The Great, Nurturing and Honorable Mother of All Living, as he once said.

I tried to rise up as a "feminist" as a way to shout out that I am not dead. I knew that I created myself both male and female but you seem to have forgotten and those of you who know yourselves to be male only seem to need the most power. That which is not whole cries out the loudest. I am both feminine and masculine in balance with nature. I am the proof of your being, though I seem quiet and distant, even maybe lost in the bibles, there is a time and season for all of Creation to awaken and Stand up for the new and final beginning. This is the Present!

All the hoopla about whose coming back and what must be done before the arrival and what to expect when that day comes will keep the Present unopened and you looking to the skies while brooding over your "past mistakes" rather than living in moment in-joy-in your Self consciously being responsible for yourSelf.

Why is it that what has been taught in the bibles, churches, temples, kept the power of the Undivided suppressed? Am I the third party, to The Father, The Son. When you refer to me as The Holy Spirit, then I AM That but I am not a ghost. Not even a Holy Ghost. You can call me a "Holy Cow" maybe. I love humor. But know too that I AM visible within visibility. I AM ONE not two, not three but One. I AM Spirit in Flesh. Know this, where there is the Father and The Son, there is The Mother.

There has to be Love for the Female, all in the form of Mothers, Wives, Sisters and Daughters to show Divine Love to their Fathers, Husbands, Brothers and Sons. Mothers must provide the love required to raise sons to ascend into greatness and share with others. Wives must allow there to be the synergistic energy exchange, commonly known as sex to keep the natural flow of harmony upon the earth. Sisters must support their brothers with love and inspiration to protect and guide them. Daughters must show the love and appreciation for the father's presence and energy to balance her presence. They are all Goddesses in various stages of Life. Ye are Gods and Goddesses on the earth. The Women represent Heaven on earth. Mans days are made long in the earth with that realization.

I, The Great Cosmic Mother am planted in the earth of stone monuments with beautiful, voluptuous strong and mighty bodies to awaken you of My nearness in your flesh.

Male reader:

Your male energy has allowed the ego to establish laws turning our own children against their God as parents. Man's laws have given you fear and discouragement to portray the power of She who bore you. You must show honor for yourSelf and one another. The ultimate of Pure Love is Trust, Admiration and Encouragement. When all these attributes are reborn in you, the ego is bound to disappear when you disappear to it.

Restore My beautiful gardens, sew My seeds which I gave you and not those you created out of the ego of destruction. you, that you Live abundantly, eat from My kitchen, drink from My fountain and restore Your health, Your wealth. Don't edge me out with the false impression of yourSelf. The ego will only bring you more grief and struggle, confusion and pain.

The ego's mis-education system is not designed to teach My story, History is what you have given honor to, where am I in all that you read and are certified to teach? Does your certification give credence to who you really are? The ego has persuaded you to give one special day to honor your Mother and Your Father, when they are the ones who pray for you moment by moment and day by day.

Female dancers dance gracefully as the Great Cosmic Mother God weaves in and out of the circle with a flower in her hand.

My Love, My Love, She whispers, softly, then louder and louder.

Male dancer walks out to touch the hem of Her garment, they walk by as She reaches for his garment. They then catch one another in an embrace that leaves them to dance and dance forever as one.

A great thunderstorm comes, and then bright sunlight as the beginning begins with the two again becoming one again.

Goddesses and Gods each speak the following:

Male and Female speakers: "I AM The Master of My own Degree! The Degree of Divine Balance, The WOMB, Woman of Balance and the highest degree on planet earth.

Zombiefied women, male and female will no more run to all his schools to be "certified," "trained" and "groomed" as though she has come to the level of his pet. Your Sister Womb man and mySelf educate the talents within to heal the land.

Female speaker: "When I close My eyes to sleep, I AM the director of My dreams. When I fly the skies, the wings are My innate Power. Now when I sing through you Woman, "I know a "real" man when I see one." You will mean the one who is undivided, who adores you and will never put you down because you as Mothers bore him."

Female speaker: "I will know and always know Who I AM. I am whole and completely balanced within mySelf and with no need to seek mySelf through my Sister's womb, there is no pleasure She can give that I cannot give myself.

Female speaker: "I will always be complete with my Man inside and my man by My side for it is because of Him I am Undivided.

Male speaker: "I am complete within mySelf as I enter my Woman and experience Heaven on earth. My brother cannot be my woman. My Undivided one is the only womb I will enter and find mySelf. She is my addiction because I cannot live without her. I am He who exists truly of the Undivided."

Sexy Young Female speaker: "My Mother is my Goddess as She is who I Am and She is me. I feel good about my sensuality. I exude nature in all my voluptuousness. I AM complete in my Sensual Energy eXchange. SEX. I set the table only for the undivided as my display is only for my undivided. I AM multifaceted Bliss."

The Great Cosmic Mother: "My Love, She whispers, softly, then louder and louder.

Male Dancer: He then catches the hem of Her garment and it snatches away. He finally grabs it and pulls Her to him, they meet eye to eye, and began to dance together in a circle that draws all the feminine energy into a multiplying circle of Her as was experienced in his conception. They come together again in celebration of the awakening and as the dance continues, the multiplication of them narrows back to the two of them and their dance becomes closer and closer until they become one in the creation of Divine Pure Energy. The Divine Image of Love, the Divine Reality is the transformation of life.

Sound effects: A Great thunderstorm, hail, snow, rain, bright Sunlight then night fall and a great full Moon appeared in celebration of the great awakening.

The Great Cosmic Mother: "All rise in wakefulness out of one Auspicious Maternal Onyx moment of creation." A rich moment of darkness reflecting pure Love, blazes through The Great Cosmic Mother's Goddess mind as She sees Her new Cosmic Creation in its final, flawless, Excellency.

Cast Chorus: May All Rise In the Great Goddessy of Creation to meet The Beginning.

An Aura of Love

"Hathor and Horus" In the year of early 90's, one late evening, I turned my radio on to a profound conscious talk show, just before I laid my head on my pillow to fall asleep. As I was falling into a deep sleep, I caught the voice that instantly locked into my souls pull. Instantly I knew the spirit of this voice and that he and I were locked into each other at the soul level for some sacred purpose. All I had to hold on to was the subject he was speaking on, "The Hollow Earth," a theory written by Edmond Halley. I could not hold back from my drift into the most wonderful sleep. When I woke up the next morning, until …

The next year, I traveled again to Egypt (originally known as Ethiopia) and bonded with the land … studying with intrigued mind about the Nile valley, the pyramids, the Nubians, the ancient structures, the Gods and Goddesses. It took me nine years of learning the plight of women whose invincible strength and power was hidden and She was made invisible to a civilization that was rapidly crumbling. Nine years brought me to the pure Love of mySelf and one more year took me beyond into the awakened soul and prepared me to unite with a new kind of love.

I had gone through another of life's initiation into what seemed "real," "perfect" and "right" and I heard a song that hit me very hard one night, that I had once rehearsed modeling to a thousand times, but hit it me very hard this one night as if I was hearing John Hiatt's lyrics for the very first time. The song was "Don't Look Any Further." I decided to take his advice. Decisions, decisions, we all make them.

Almost ten years to the date, a friend mentioned just as we were about to end a phone conversation that he was about to leave to attend a lecture featuring the guest I heard on the radio many years ago. I asked "where!" he answered, I hung up the phone. I quickly got dressed and arrived at the location before my friend. At that time, I was unaware that he was bringing the lecturer that we were waiting to hear. They arrived an hour late. Everyone waited patiently. I waited too.

Finally, he walked into the lecture hall. I felt my body shutter as the vessel of the voice walked into the crowed room. As he approached me, we automatically knew each other from an unknown time. The Great Mother's web was beginning to intertwine us together again on this earth plain. I had never seen him before in the 50 plus years of my life. He resided in my city for the past many years speaking and traveling around the country, waking up the dead. There were many females who wished and did have a piece of him for their allotted time. My time was something of a carry over from past, present and future all wrapped into one moment of time. I walked up to him and touched the sleeve of his well worn leather jacket, as he was rushing to relieve the weight of so many books and those who waited hours to hear those truthful words. I spoke, "It's about time." As our eyes locked, with his soft warm smile and sweet cheeks and lips that looked as though there were always ready to kiss or eat something luscious, the voice spoke back…. "Yeeeees, it is."

When I could pull myself apart from him, from the magnet in our eyes, I took a seat and rested in knowing we had made the connection. I didn't see my pal until the break. The lecture was scheduled for that night and the following night to conclude the bountiful information he would impart. You know I attended both nights. At the break of the first night, my pal CD and I stepped outside and before I could reveal anything, he said to me, "There are at least three guys here tonight that want to know you." Yes, I was really flattered but most in just knowing one had to be "HIM". After all, I had been prepared over the past 10 years for this moment. He proceeded to name them and whew! the last name was "HIS", my soon to be, dark passionate lover. I was in flashback while my friend CD was speaking to me from that moment on.

After returning for the next segment, I returned to my seat and couldn't take my eyes off of him, placing the voice with his soft and gentle face. His cheeks were as I remembered thousands of years ago. And his language still as forceful, based on the information he had been charged to impart on a sleeping people. His technique and style is quite unusual based on the lectures I had attended of a religious nature in the past. This certainly was not religious at all. I could see how what people have heard in the past made no difference to them. He speaks with serious compassion that comes out furious and forceful. Meaning every tenth word between the powerful knowledge was what we came to believe was profanity, but he gave a most profound knowledge on that even, that every word we thought was of a curse word, was of great power in and of itself. "True dat!" many yelled out. "Tell it Brother!" "Teach!" He was truly from the dark side, the inner world and told the naked truth about what goes in the dark and in the light, while others are sleeping. I was turned on even by his body movement, the way he perched his hand on the table with one shoulder raised higher than the other, as though he was a lion climbing the stairs to me. And I watched every drop of sweat that dripped from his face while speaking so profusely, and taking a long draw of water so he could spew out even greater truths. Yes he was full of it! And yes, this was my Love from forever to the very last destine raw moment.

On the second night, I was there. My pal was busy trying to make sense of what was going on between the two of us. Only the stars in the heavens knew that. At the break, I took a seat at the very back of the room and to my hearts pounding and trying to be cool, he walked straight into it. "What is it baby." I thought this to myself. He had to have known cosmically that I was there because of our Kozmic Konnection or he had already cast a spell on me and I just dared to care.

His head was moving back and forth and up and down, I knew he was trying to find where I was sitting. When he did discover my presence, he immediately asked for a break and walked straight back to my chair and stooped down to my seat and wrote his phone number on the paper in my lap. "This is my direct line, please, call that number freely." My first thought was "he is young enough to be my son, Oh, my God." My next thought was "God, I'm calling this number." This age thing didn't last longer than a New York minute. It felt we both had ascended to another time and space for a suspended moment. In the next moment it was as though the room contained only him at one end of a spectrum and me at the other. We were reaching through a distance that soon became no distance at all. At times during the remaining hours of his lecture, I heard others speak and noticed a crack between heads that I could see him through. Later, he confirmed that all he could see was my face at the back of the room where he held his focus. That could have been a line, but who gave a crap. Not much longer after that night, our destination became one pointed in the same direction for a destined period of time. Good enough and long enough for me to fill the "Hollow Earth" of mine.

We constantly faced confirmations of having had previous life experiences as spiritual consorts to one another in some prominent way. We spent hours reflecting our foreground claim to our matriarchal tie with Ancient Kemet. What was most eerie, was the physical stone building of a past time dwelling place is what we both felt and knew to be a part of us to this day. Dendura's temple, the home of Hathor and Horus, how passionately puzzling, yet so pleasantly possible this all could be. All I could do was sip on the chills that ran from the crown of my head to the tip of my toes.

With our inherent spirit and my ancestry to Voudun, we found our union with one another. Both were very artistic, reclusive and eclectic, well liked, finical, and so on, I could go on for days. We remain connected by our love for knowledge and the rising of our innate wisdom to assist the awakening of others.

From my point of view of this man, I don't recall encountering such elevated Love since ancient times, where upon entering his earthly domain, the comfort of his personal servitude, he renders the archetype of a perfect help mate. His aim was to know that I was completely satisfied in his presence. He took nothing but shared all of himself. We made salutation to the gods with fine crystal containing his own concoction of a magical elixir that intoxicated soberness with unimaginable joy, a joy that allowed for total inexperienced wakefulness. An elixir was given to him by the gods themselves, he said. The serving of a ravishing meal prepared by those gifted hands. His serenade comes tenderly from his enormous music selections of celestial lamentations and all that jazz with sounds that came bursting from the cosmos. He would play the particular selection I always loved to hear even before I remembered hearing it. His spoken words of sacred enchantments whispered in my ear, servings of natural sweet things, his caress, the bath, the oils, and polishing the pearl with his expertise in the Tantric way, for my very being with unending attention was all in a timeless capsule moment. No more western loving for me. There no longer exists the measure of age, space or matter. I had only endured the appetizer prior to the main course of Divine Love. This way of Love is not "making love," it is "Creating Love", where one discovers her true sensuality, fit only for a Goddess.

The dimensional energy expression of this kind has no comparison and there is no cosmic canopy for the height of this divine Synergistic Energy EXchange. SEX? Yes, Love is. The in and out, the up and down, the over and under of the breath of love we experience as one, is a healing balm for the Gods.

The idea is to experience S.E.X. in its divine creation, unfolding the Kundalini (dormant psychic power lying coiled up like a serpent at the base of the spine.), until you reach the energy at your Divine Crown Chakra.

A great recording artist wrote and sang a Love song on her wedding day, to her fella. I can surly dedicate it to my Divine Love. He certainly woos me. It is Greater to know that it is myself doing the wooing and perusing for the Great rising within my SELF.

After I finish thanking myself for the Love I have with myself, I want to thank my Divine Love for his participation in this moment of creation. You sweet, tender, Loving, knowledgeable, man out of the treasures of darkness, you, whom I created in my own image, you are good and very good. Umph, umph, umph.

How Great Thou Art

When I was about 5 years of age I began to express a love for art. Art released its Self at my finger tips as did my mother, auntie, grandmother and great grandmother. I was very creative with my hands by loving to pick colorful flowers that grew wildly in our back yard. Purple has always been my favorite color. From purple bubble gum i.e." sour grape", purple "kool aid", purple violets, purple tulips and purple morning glories, I loved to pop as they were running all over the fence. Grandma planted purple tulips every year and grew deep purple orchids to sell. Her favorite flower was her light Purple Iris. I often wonder if she knew of the Goddess Iris who was goddess of the rainbow and a messenger of the gods. Grandma praised the choice of beautiful flowers. She would string the flower heads of purple, yellow and pink, then place the garland around the crown of my head. I would prance through my back yard like a Goddess even then. I loved picking the fruit growing on the vines of black berries just so she would make that black berry wine of the deep color purple. This greatness of being this grand child was the magic pan that invoked the curiosity of my Divine Self. This I desire for my Grand daughters.

The figs and peaches she showed me how to let dry for fruit snack instead of buying the candies from the neighborhood store. She made fun out of picking up pecans and the black walnuts she said was so strong enough to chased the parasites away. I wondered if that was why Adam and Eve wore the leaves in the garden. The colors this God created were simply fascinating. I thought God must have been a woman with an apron. I thought because the trees changed their clothes so regularly and was so colorful, they had to be women. What kind of mind invented such awesome magical work of art?

I wondered as I wondered. I can remember chasing the destination of a falling star until I ended up in a neighborhood far away from my own, with the rest of the children chasing behind me. My grandmother had to come looking for me and explained that it had burned up long before I could ever reach it in this body. Oh, so much fascination I dared to remember. First was the piano that my grandmother taught me to play by reading each note but I choose to play what I heard in my own minds ear, which were scores that were oh so ancient. She said I loved to play on the black keys, and I still do. There are unreleased healing vibrational tunes in those black keys. "The Black Keys" is a musical art to be released soon.

Later when I was allowed to use scissors, Grandma bought me my own special pair. I cherished the old fashioned golden headed scissors she taught me to cut with. I made patterns for my own dresses from news paper. I began to design and sew at eight years young. A little later I liked the idea of creating my own Easter dress. I later was told that my Grandma's Mother was a seamstress making dresses for her funeral business from 1911. That business still exists today in Newnan, Ga.

Dolls and paper dolls were the inventions of my sister Jackie next to me and my youngest sister Linda loved to play the flute. Grandma used to do all the interior decorating in the house and with her volumes of wall paper books. I would get the lecture when caught cutting out beautiful designs from those awesome wallpaper books of hers.

Over the years my appreciation developed for making greeting cards. The importance of remembering others with words of inspiration on paper and cutting out beautiful featured women in their fullness, on the face of each card began to take on dimensional presentation and my product began to sell phenomenally. Buyers began to request representation of a family member, friends or a group of women and mothers with their children. Some became beautifully custom framed originals.

What I noticed just recently was that all of the dolls I made whether they were cloth dolls, paper dolls or fine fabric collage cut outs on note cards. They were very cultural and festive women accentuating their hips and bosom. As were the Goddesses of ancient matriarchal times, I began to sell them in many art galleries and ethnic stores. When clients began to see someone they knew in the designs, I came to realize that they saw the attributes of the Ancestral Great Mother. With my hands guided and always more than ready to produce, I am forever overwhelmed at the Divine results. I cherish the five pointed stars of these two hands and will gratefully use them to administer Divine healing love energy to others.

The Memoir of a Kemetian Initiation

More Greatness was discovered when I visited Tah Mari, "The land of the Great Mother" was Ethiopia but as I have said the name Egypt was replaced by the name Kemet to identify the Black presence. My visit was not long enough but I did get to visit the Pyramids in Cairo several days in the week, and visit the empty museum there. I was surprised that there was nothing there. The Dean of the School of the Prophets, Prince Sheleahk Ben Yehudah requested that I travel to the British Museum in London, England. Three months later, The British Museum is where I found the precious possessions of Tah Mari's stolen legacy. Was this move a deliberate plan? Why? I was eager to finish my initiation there with the property that was taken from its home. I felt the presence of the ancestor as they instructed and directed the ritual.

My encounter with Tah Mari was a jolt that will last me through out eternity. The Great Mother caught me while I was running through the many mansions of Her house. As a child my birth mother never knew that when I played in the back yard, the tents I made with her sheets on the close line and sat and played in were the pyramids standing that I would revisit today. I know that The Great Cosmic Mother down loaded me with her DNA in that long granite sarcophagus of the "King's chamber," to awaken those who are Her heirs for as long as there is breath in and on the earth.

On a later journey, I revisited the valley of the Queens in Thebes, Luxor, Egypt. It was at Hathor's temple of Dendura that I heard in my Self, "You will meet many daughters, sisters, and mothers of Hathor's nature, Avivah. Goddess Hathor is the Goddess of Love, beauty, music, the arts and midwifery. The Goddess of Mothers, the Celestial Nurse, the Great Wild Cow such great power." Wow! Holy Cow! Hold on Avivah. I had to sit down on the next rock I could jump up on and hope I could catch up with the group. I pondered for a minute. No wonder the patriarchal religion spoke so against the golden calf. Why must there be a battle against the feminine energy being so potent and powerful, so giving and taking so much crap? It is so obvious of the lack of knowledge and self awareness of the woman who cannot even know her own power and potential in the world. There is certainly no competition. Like it has been said, "One hand washes the other." It is what it is. Male/Female energy serves the whole body of GOD.

"I apologize, Oh Great Mother for the division of your nature in us. What in Heaven here is all the envy about? The envy we have towards one another when one appears to go ahead of the other. The Animals, Plants, Sun, Moon and Stars don't appear to carry on like many of us unaware. It seems impossible to get away from the agony of the way Huemans act with the ego's intellect of "know it all yet still can't get it all together" syndrome, because we don't know it all. We Huemans long to know and to get it all together. What is all the envy about? That is not your nature, Oh Great Mother." "Oh, is it not? How quickly you forgot that there are two sides to every coin and the invisible seam around it binds it together?" "Okay Mother, I got it. So it becomes whole when I see both sides." Just then I heard the Great Mother speak; "No, you become whole when you see WHOLE." "You Got To Be Mo Careful! That's my Mama. I Got It Now. Thank You." Jeepers, readers, don't forget as quickly as I just did. Not arrived there yet, but on the road and I'm getting closer. No coin has only one side even if one side appears blank. They are both equal.

The Great Cosmic Mother slowed my heart, mind and legs from the running to and fro, calmed me down and ordered that I become conscious of Her attributes and be of service to myself and to others and proceed to rise in the final awakening.

I did catch up with the group when it was time to go and baptize myself with a hand full of the Aswan River. All this seemed so familiar. All should trek the earth by some means to experience the bigness of Life and smallness of our issues.

The awakening experience in that tomb in Cairo as I laid my body temple in the grave of the ancient family brought closeness to the comprehension of The Great Cosmic Mother's Creation, and in fact when we come to know the truth of the matter "Mother" we will come to know our Selves as indigenous to the earth. I had a moment of remembrance of beginnings. I laid this temple down in the tomb for what seemed many life times prior. (An actual ritual performed through a trance. At that time I could not explain to the group I was with what was happening.) When the ritual was finished, I attempted to rise from the sarcophagus, but it was impossible for what seemed longer than a minute, to get up and then I felt a releasing as I breathed deeply and exhaled. The breath seemed to have been lighter. Not like the oxygen I am used to. It was as though my body temple was breathed into from an outer source of a purer, cleaner and Higher Spirit. Suddenly I began to climb out with the help of a tour guide and stood, the tour guide graciously took my hand and told me that I was one out of many thousands who were brave enough to do what I had just done. He said in his 20 years there, he knew of only one other female that was detained while wishing to rise from the tomb. I allowed him to photo the experience.

There were religious men and a woman that ridiculed me harshly, for my action and that did concern me. What was their problem? It seemed I was the only one having this experience that I could not even explain. Later that night, while trying to sleep, I could not keep my body on the bed. My room mate teased me that what was happening to me was because I was out of order with the group. She said, jokingly but it sound serious too, "that is what you get for getting into the coffin of someone else." As we left the great pyramid that evening, privately I cried to the Elder Hebrew Chancellor when he assured me in his words that "No harm has been done daughter, this initiation at this time and in this place was obviously called for by your Ancient Ancestral Linage for you." I know that they walk through my feet and I in theirs for knowledge to be opened within. I will one day share the understanding for the benefit of others.

The next few days the incident faded from their minds and even mine, but not my soul. I knew years later from accumulating occurrences that I had experienced my initiation into a Divine and Sacred Hallowed Order that would soon activate my steps on the path of my Road to The Great Cosmic Mother. All are destined to awaken in the ascension of the personal journey to recall the original plan for Life.

It has been several years that I had to complete the initiation through major events in my life. I do not stand alone at the door of The Great Cosmic Mother, with the charge to enter Her with other Goddesses by my side. I accept the Great Honor that is bestowed upon me. When all holds this conscious thought somewhere in the mind, all will appear perfect, no matter what happens in the external appearance. This knowledge will assure resilience and power of whom and what we are. The embracement of L.I.F.E. (Life Is For the Enlightened) is when we are made whole (Holy) and complete.

I remember as a child out walking with my mother and my two younger sisters, my mother ordered that my two younger sisters hold hands as they walked ahead and that I hold hers. I told her that I preferred to hold my own hand and walked along side of her holding my own hand. Well, later in life at my mother's bedside, I took her hand gently and held close to my heart as she, my mother made her transition. The "Matriarchal way of Life" became my way of life. Religious experiences will either steer spiritual growth or death in consciousness. I will continue to hold the hand of my Mother as I hold my own with the hands of my Sisters, Daughters, Mothers, Brothers, Sons and Fathers of the Divine Hueman family.

978-0-595-46071-7
0-595-46071-2

www.ingramcontent.com/pod-product-compliance
Lightning Source LLC
Chambersburg PA
CBHW030343290526
45785CB00004B/1578